GOD the FATHER
meditations for the millennium

GOD the FATHER
meditations for the millennium

MARK LINK

ThomasMore®
– An RCL Company –
ALLEN, TEXAS

IMPRIMI POTEST
Bradley M. Schaeffer, S.J.

NIHIL OBSTAT
Rev. Msgr. Glenn D. Gardner, J.C.D.
Censor Librorum

IMPRIMATUR
† Most Rev. Charles V. Grahmann
Bishop of Dallas

April 27, 1998

The Nihil Obstat and Imprimatur are official declarations that the material reviewed is free of doctrinal or moral error. No implication is contained therein that those granting the Nihil Obstat and Imprimatur agree with the contents, opinions, or statements expressed.

ACKNOWLEDGMENT

Unless otherwise noted, all Scripture quotations are from Today's English Version text. Copyright © American Bible Society 1966, 1971, 1976, 1992. Used by permission.

Cover photo: Photodisc

Copyright 1998 Mark Link

All rights reserved. No part of this book shall be reproduced or transmitted in any form or by any means, electronic or mechanical, including photocopying, recording, or by any information or retrieval system, without written permission from the Publisher.

Send all inquiries to:

Thomas More®
An RCL Company
200 East Bethany Drive
Allen, Texas 75002–3804

Toll Free   800–264–0368
Fax   800–688–8356

Vision 2000 on Internet—http://v2000.org

Printed in the United States of America

Library of Congress Catalog Card Number: 98–060986

7423   ISBN 0–88347–423–9

1 2 3 4 5   02 01 00 99 98

Contents

Search for the Father

Week 1 Inner Longing — 8

Touch of the Father

Week 2 Graced Moments — 16
Week 3 Critical Tests — 24

Word of the Father

Week 4 Love Story — 32
Week 5 Cosmic Word — 40
Week 6 Cosmos & Scientists — 48
Week 7 Cosmos & Religion — 56
Week 8 Inspired Word — 64
Week 9 Incarnate Word — 72

Plan of the Father

Week 10 Jesus' Calling — 80
Week 11 Our Calling — 88

Faith in the Father

Week 12 Call to Trust — 96
Week 13 An Ongoing Journey — 104

Presence of the Father

Week 14 Different Ways — 112

Prayer to the Father

Week 15 Meditation — 120
Week 16 Contemplation — 128
Week 17 Conversation — 136
Week 18 The Psalms — 144
Week 19 The Lord's Prayer–1 — 152
Week 20 The Lord's Prayer–2 — 160

Father! [Abba] my Father!

One summer day in Israel,
scripture scholar Dorothy Dawes
was watching a group of Israeli children
cool off in the Sea of Galilee.
Suddenly, a child in the water called out
to his Father on the shore, *"Abba!"*

This ancient word caught her by surprise.
It also moved her deeply.
Abba was the word Jesus used
to invoke the Father in the great crisis
of his life in the garden of Gethsemane.
Mark 14:36

Literally, the word *Abba* means "Daddy."
It connotes the kind of loving trust
that a two-year-old has
as she climbed up and sat on her daddy's lap.

Early Christians followed Jesus' example.
They, too, invoked God
under the affectionate title of *Abba*.
Thus we read in the Letter to the Romans:

*The Spirit
makes you God's children,
and by the Spirit's power
we cry out to God,
"Father! [Abba] my Father!"*
Romans 8:15

Addressing God in this affectionate way
contrasts dramatically with the
Old Testament way of addressing God.
In all of the Old Testament the word "Father"
is used of God less than 25 times.
And never is the title *Abba* applied to God.

With the coming of Jesus
in New Testament times, all this changes.
The title "Father" becomes
the preferred way of addressing God.
It appears more than 250 times
in the the writings of the New Testament.

Meditations for the Millennium—God the Father uses a story approach
to try to deepen our appreciation of God—
the same God whom the Spirit empowers us
to address affectionately as *Abba*.

Let us begin our spiritual journey
with this thought:

> *It is the heart
> that experiences God,
> not the reason.*
> Blaise Pascal

Week 1 — *Search for the Father*

Inner longing

One day, a young lady asked James Martin,
"How can I find God?"
She had lost touch with her church,
but not with the hunger for God
in her heart.

It kept badgering her
at the most unexpected times and
in the most unexpected places:
driving to work, watching a game,
or sitting momentarily in the dark,
after turning off the 10 o'clock news.

The young lady
is typical of many people today.
They are among the brightest
of our generation.
They are bright enough to know
how to be successful in their occupation.
But they are also bright enough to know
that there is more to life
than being successful in one's occupation.

Like the young lady, an "inner longing"
for God keeps badgering them.

And so, this "inner longing" prompted Martin
to ask a wide rainbow of people
this question:

*If someone were to ask you,
"How can I find God?"
what would you say?
I asked them to imagine the questioner
as a close friend,
who had no specific religious affiliation.*
How Can I Find God? Liguori Missouri, 1997

The people Martin interviewed
came from different religious traditions:
Jewish, Catholic, Protestant, and Muslim.

They were also from
a wide range of occupational backgrounds:
factory workers, politicians, poor people,
young mothers, lawyers, and theologians.

Martin explained why he interviewed people
from such a wide range of backgrounds.
He said:

*My belief is
that God is at work in everyone's life,
and therefore,
the comments of a young mother
or a corporation lawyer, or prison inmate
are as meaningful as those of a theologian,
minister, sister, priest, rabbi.* Ibid

This week's meditations focus on
the "inner longing" or hunger
that leads people
to embark on a search for the Father.

Why this inner longing in my heart?

*As the deer longs
for a stream of cool water,
so I long for you, O God.* Psalms 42:1

The human heart was born
with a "longing" or "hunger" for God.
How did this longing get into the heart?
In his book, *Man Does Not Stand Alone*,
A. Cressy Morrison cites an example
that points to a possible answer.
He tells how eels swim thousands of miles
from Europe and America to Bermuda.
There they breed, give birth and die.
Then, some instinct or "inner longing"
prompts their offspring to swim back across
the same ocean in search of the river or lake
from which their parent came.
The eel's "inner longing" for its true "home"
is not unlike the "inner longing"
that leads the heart to search for its "home."
But the heart's home is not a "place."
It's a "person"—the God who created it
and put the "inner longing" in the heart.

How do I experience a longing for God?

*Follow the longing in your heart
as gladly as Wise Men followed the star
to the stable in Bethlehem.
The longing in your heart
will, also, lead you to Jesus.*

Journal

Week I   Day two

Journal

I ask myself, 'Is there really a God?'

I looked for him, but couldn't find him;
I called to him, but heard no answer.
Song of Songs 4:6

From his youth, Fulton Oursler searched for a satisfying answer to the question: "Is there really a God?"
He couldn't understand why other people weren't as concerned about the answer as he was.
In his adult years his search continued, but with no answer.
Then, one day, in sheer desperation, he walked into St. Patrick's in New York, knelt down, and prayed in words like this:
"Ten minutes from now I may change my mind and scoff at what I am doing now.
Pay no attention to me then.
Right now I am in my right mind and heart.
This is my best—take it.
If you are there, help me."
That prayer proved to be the first step on the road that guided him "home."
It led him to a deep, fruitful faith in God that lasted all of his life.

What started me on my journey home?
How deep and fruitful is my faith in God?

You are a child of God.
Please call home. Bumper sticker

How do I begin to search for God?

*Listen! I stand at the door and knock;
if any hear my voice and open the door,
I will come into their house.* Revelation 3:20

Avery Dulles was the son
of John Foster Dulles, Secretary of State
under President Eisenhower.
A highly respected theologian,
he writes:
"The search for God
can appropriately begin from a reflection
on the voice of conscience.
Anyone who has experienced
the fact of moral obligation
has the makings of a belief in God
and has the prerequisites
for hearing God's word fruitfully.
But the hearing of that word
will not result in faith
unless it is accompanied by prayer.
quoted in *How Can I Find God*, edited by James Martin

Why might "the search for God" begin from
a reflection on the voice of conscience?
Why must it be accompanied by prayer?

*Two things fill the mind
with ever-new and increasing
wonder and awe—
the starry heavens above me
and the moral law within me.* Immanuel Kant

Journal

Week 1   Day four

Journal

How does conscience impact my search for God?

*Eli realized that it was the LORD
who was calling the boy, so he said . . .
"If he calls you again, say,
'Speak, LORD, your servant is listening.'"*
1 Samuel 3:8–9

John Henry Newman writes:
"Conscience praises, it blames, it promises,
it threatens, it implies a future
and it witnesses to the unseen.
It is more than man's own self.
The man himself has no power over it,
or only with extreme difficulty;
he may not make it, he cannot destroy it,
he may refuse to use it, but it remains. . . .
Its very existence
throws us out of ourselves,
to go seek him . . . whose Voice it is."
Apologia Pro Vita Sua

When and how do I experience
the inner voice that drives me
to seek the one whose Voice it is?

*Every person, however good,
has yet a better person within them.
When the outer person
is unfaithful to his deeper convictions,
the person within whispers a protest.
The name of this whisper in the soul
is conscience.* Friedrich Von Humboldt

How do I know the Father's voice?

Lord, teach us to pray. Luke 11:1

Fulton Oursler was a prominent author
and a senior editor of *Reader's Digest*.
Reflecting on his spiritual journey,
he said: "It is through prayer
that we know there is a God . . .
Through prayer we know God—as Father. . . .
As we come to know God,
the urge to serve God personally
becomes overpowering.
We must feed the hungry, visit the sick . . .
clothe the naked . . .
That is where the human being
comes closest to God and knows God best.
Isn't it strange that
it should have taken me so many years
to find the key to the mystery? . . .
I have much lost time to make up."
Liberty, March 1949

What role do prayer and service
play in my own quest for
a personal relationship with God?

Two people please God—
who serves him with all his heart,
because he knows God;
and one who seeks him with all his heart
because he knows God not.
Panin

Week 1 — Day six

Journal

Where can I find my Father today?

"I was sick and you took care of me." Matthew 25:36

William Simon
was the Secretary of the Treasury
under Presidents Nixon and Ford,
He was also a eucharistic minister
in his own church.
This means he brought Holy Communion
to hospital patients and infirm people.
While doing this, something happened to him
that he hadn't anticipated. He writes:
"Many times I have come away
from the hospital wondering if I have given
the sick and infirm
half of what they've given me. . . .
I feel profoundly grateful to them
for helping me to strengthen my faith."
He concludes by saying that when people ask,
"Where can we find God in today's world?"
One answer is: "Almost anywhere—
in fact, many times right in front of us,
if we just open our eyes and hearts."
How Can I Find God: James Martin, editor

Where have I been searching for God
in today's world? With what results?

*I give you the end of a Golden String.
Only wind it into a ball—
It will lead you to heaven's gate.* William Blake

Father, teach me how to find you

Journal

*Very early the next morning,
long before daylight,
Jesus got up and left the house.
He went out of town to a lonely place,
where he prayed.* Mark 1:35

"O Lord my God, teach my heart
where and how to look for you,
where and how to find you. . . .
O Lord, you are my God . . .
and I have never seen you.
You have made me and remade me,
and you have given me
all the good things I have,
and still I do not know you.
Teach me to seek you and when I seek you
show yourself to me
for I cannot seek you unless you teach me
or find you unless you show yourself to me.
Let me look for you in my longing;
let me long for you in my looking."
Anselm of Canterbury, *Proslogion* (12th century)

How deeply do I long to pray to God?
How faithfully do I turn to God
in prayer on a regular basis?
What stumbling blocks do I experience
in my efforts to remain faithful?

*Pray to God simply, with a heart of faith.
He is your friend.* Bunjiro

Graced moments

Sir Alister Hardy was
an internationally-known marine biologist.
He also had a deep faith in God.
That faith was nourished in his youth
by his love and reverence for nature.
He writes:

*I especially liked
walking along the banks of various streams
watching, as summer developed,
the sequence of wild flowers . . .
I wandered along their banks, at times
almost with a feeling of ecstasy. . . .*

*Occasionally,
when I was sure no one could see me . . .
I fell on my knees . . . thanking God,
who felt so very real to me,
for the glories of his kingdom
and for allowing me to feel them.*
Quoted in David Hay: *Religious Experience Today*,
Mowbray, London, 1990

As Hardy grew older,
he never forgot these experiences.
Furthermore, he encountered other people
who, also, had similar experiences.

These "moments of grace" took the form of
a burst of light in a moment of darkness,
an influx of strength in a moment of need,
an unseen presence in a moment of joy.

This prompted Hardy to do research work
in the area of "religious experience."

While he was doing this
at Manchester College in England,
other scholars
were pursuing similar research
at the University of Chicago.

Significantly,
the two research projects paralleled
and confirmed one another.

The findings showed that certain
human activities had a special capacity
to "trigger" a religious experience.
Among these activities were the following:

1. contemplating nature,
2. listening to music,
3. reading scripture,
4. reflecting quietly,
5. praying alone or with others,
6. worshipping in community.

This week's meditations
focus on examples of people like Hardy
who, at some point in their lives,
seemed to feel the "touch" of the Father.

The night held a presence

Jesus went up a hill to pray and spent the whole night there praying to God. Luke 6:12

Edwin D. Starbuck was a pioneer in the study of religious experiences. In his collection of such experiences, there's an account of a man who, one night, went for a walk and ended up on a hilltop. As he stood there under the canopy of stars, something amazing took place within him. The nearest he could come to describing it was that it was like orchestral music swelling and filling his soul until it seemed it would burst from his own emotion. All the while the "perfect stillness . . . held a presence that was all the more felt because it was not seen."
He added, "I could not any more have doubted that *He* was there than that I was. Indeed, I felt myself to be, if possible, the less real of the two. My highest faith in God and truest idea of God were then born in me."
Cited by William James in *The Varieties of Religious Experience:*

What impact does inspiring music or a star-filled sky have on my spirit?

Music is well said to be the speech of angels. Thomas Carlyle

Week 2   Day two

Journal

The experience touched my soul

*The sun shines down on everything,
and everything is filled
with the Lord's glory.* Sirach 42:16

A distraught man stood on the edge
of a cliff in Italy with suicide on his mind.
Suddenly, he heard music so pure
that it startled him. He looked around.
What he saw amazed him.
There at the entrance to a cave
stood a barefoot boy playing a harmonica.
The sound of the music and
the sight of the boy
touched the depths of his soul.
Suddenly, he realized how much loveliness
and beauty were in the world.
He said later that
the barefoot boy playing the harmonica
was a gift from God. It was much more.
It was the presence and the power of God
entering his life to help him
at a time when he couldn't help himself.

Can I recall when the sight or the sound
of something beautiful touched me?

*God sent His singers upon earth
With songs of sadness and mirth,
That they might touch the hearts of men
And bring them back to heaven again.*
Henry Wadsworth Longfellow

Day three — Week 2

I knew what I heard was true

Jesus said, "Those who believe in me will never be thirsty." John 6:35

A certain young woman
admitted that she was not very religious.
Still, she considered herself
to be as good as many other people
who called themselves Christians.
One night she attended a lecture on
Christianity. She walked out of it in a daze.
"If this is true," she said to herself,
"I've got to make some radical changes."
When she got home,
she began to read the New Testament.
She said later:
"At about 1 a.m.
I knew something had happened:
no voices from heaven
but this kind of deep-down certainty
that what I had heard was true."
She underwent a remarkable conversion,
became a missionary, and now experiences
"tremendous joy and satisfaction"
in her new life.

What is there in my life, right now,
that falls short of Jesus' teaching?

*All that I am
I owe to Jesus Christ, who is revealed
to me in His divine Book.* David Livingston

Journal

Week 2 — Day four

The joy could come only from the Father

*I thank God every time I think of you . . .
I am glad and share my joy with you all.
In the same way, you must be glad
and share your joy with me.*
Philippians 1:4, 2:17–18

"It was a peaceful evening.
My mom and brother and sister and I
were on our way
to a high school basketball game . . .
It was quiet in the car. . . .
I was just looking out the window
at the still night, enjoying the stars . . .
happy to be on my way to the game.
The happiness that I was feeling
grew deeper and . . . I noticed that tears
were rolling down my cheeks.
This was really weird. . . . Then I understood.
This was how full joy could be . . .
a joy that comes only from God."
Jacques Braman, quoted in *How Can I Find God*

When did I experience a joy that appeared
to come only from God? Why? What?

*To pursue joy is to lose it.
The only way to get it
is to hold steadily to the path of duty,
without thinking of joy, and then,
like sheep, it comes most surely . . . .
to meet us.* Alexander MacLaren

Journal

We all felt
the presence of God

*Jesus said, "Where two or three
come together in my name,
I am there with them."* Matthew 18:20

Years ago, a plane carrying a Uruguayan
rugby team crashed in the snow, high up
in the Andes mountains of South America.
Miraculously, sixteen young men survived
and lived for two months on little more
than snow water. Each day they prayed
together. During these sessions
they felt God's presence as never before.
Upon rescue, one boy spoke for all, saying:
"When one awakes in the morning
amid the silence of the mountains and
sees all around the snow-capped peaks . . .
one feels alone in the world
but for the presence of God.
For I can assure you that God is there.
We all felt it, inside ourselves."
Piers Paul Read: *Alive*

When did I let the hand of God guide me?

*Arturo was not a religious boy.
One night, however, after a prayer session,
he could be heard weeping softly .
"Pedro looked at him
and asked him why he was crying.
Arturo replied, 'Because I feel
so close to God.'"* Alive: Piers Paul Read

Journal

Week 2

Day six

Journal

Every soldier knelt in the mud

The LORD is my shepherd . . .
Even if I go through the deepest darkness,
I will not be afraid. Psalms 23:1, 4

Father Joseph Hogan was a chaplain
in Europe with the U.S. Third Army.
One Sunday he felt the presence of God
in a way that touched him deeply.
He writes:
"I was saying Mass on top of a jeep.
The men were standing there
with their guns slung over their backs and
their helmets on. The ack-ack was pecking
at the planes upstairs.
There was a torrent of rain coming down
and a sea of mud to wallow in.
So I said, 'Don't bother to kneel down.'
And they didn't, until the Consecration.
Then every man went down on his knees . . .
When they sloshed up to receive Holy Communion,
they again knelt in mud puddles."
A *do-it-yourself retreat,* Loyola University Press, 1961

When did I sense God's presence at church?

God has been profoundly real to me in recent years.
In the midst of outer dangers,
I have felt an inner calm. In the midst of
lonely days and dreary nights, I have heard
an inner voice saying, "Lo, I will be with you."
Dr. Martin Luther King, Jr., *Strength to Love,* 1963

God is a dancer; creation, the dance

Journal

*LORD . . . You are around me
on every side; you protect me
with your power.* Psalms 139:5

Disciple: Master, how I can experience
the presence and touch
of the One for whom
my heart longs.
Master: My dear disciple,
it is with deep regret
that I must tell you
I can't teach you how to do that.
Disciple: Master, I don't understand!
Why can't you teach me?
Master: For the same reason
that I can't teach
a fish swimming in a lake
how to get in touch
with the water.

How do I interpret the Master's response
to the disciple?

*God is the Dancer,
His creation is the Dance.
The dance . . . has no existence
apart from the Dancer. . . .
Be silent and look at the Dance.
Just look: a star, a flower, a fading leaf . . .
And hopefully it won't be long
before you see . . . the Dancer.* Anthony de Mello

Critical Tests

For years, a small statue of Cupid
stood in the entrance hall
of an old New York City mansion,
owned by the French embassy.

Its arms and face were badly damaged;
but it had a mysterious charm
that made it a good conversation piece.

One day it attracted the attention
of Professor Brandt of New York University.
As she studied it, her heart beat faster.
It matched the description
of a long-lost work of Michelangelo.
Further study showed that it was "Cupid,"
sculpted by him in his youth.

The story of the statue
makes a good parable of God.
Like the statue, God is present in our midst,
but unrecognized by the majority of people.

But every once in a while
someone recognizes God's presence
with the same surprise and certitude
that Professor Brandt experienced
when she recognized Cupid.

This raises a question:
How can we distinguish between
a *graced* experience with God and
an *imaginary* one?

Spiritual writers suggest three tests:

First, there is the *time test*.
Sometimes in a moment of high emotion
people report feeling the presence
of a spiritual power.

If their "feeling" is simply
the product of natural emotion, it will fade.
If, however, it is a "graced" experience
the person with be changed,
and that change will be evident over time
in what the person says and does.

Secondly, there is the *reality test*.
If a person's experience is truly "graced"
and not "imagined,"
it will lead to an increase of faith or hope.

Finally, there is the *charity test*.
When a person is blessed with
a "graced" experience,
that person will become more loving.
For instance, the person's focus
will shift away from themselves
and to God and others.

This week's meditations
focus on how such spiritual experiences
have impacted people's lives.

After that, I was never the same

*Two of Jesus' disciples were going
to a village named Emmaus . . .
Jesus himself drew near
and walked along with them.* Luke 24:13, 15

Estlin Carpenter served as visiting chaplain
from England to Harvard University.
The surprising thing about Carpenter
was that during his college days
he was apathetic about God and religion.
Then one afternoon he went for a walk,
and something unexpected happened.
He felt an incredible presence of God.
It was as real to him as if someone,
suddenly, began walking along with him,
as Jesus did with the Emmaus disciples.
That experience impacted him dramatically.
His attitude toward God and religion
did an about-face. He said,
"I could now not only believe in God with
my mind, but also love him with my heart."
Carpenter was never the same again
after that afternoon.

Why should only a few people be blessed
with such a spiritual presence?

*Our Father dwells in tents
as well as in temples,
but His favorite abiding place
is in the hearts of mankind.* J. Fred Jones

Journal

Week 3 — Day two

Journal

I knew I was in God's presence

*From the time you were born,
I have helped you.
Do not be afraid.* Isaiah 44:2

A woman wrote:
"I had an experience seven years ago
that changed my whole life.
I had lost my husband six months before
and my courage at the same time.
I felt life would be useless
if fear were allowed to govern me.
One evening with no preparation,
as sudden and dynamic
as the Revelation of Saul of Tarsus,
I knew I was in the presence of God,
and that he . . . loved me with a love
beyond imagination—no matter what I did."
Anonymous in *David Hay: Religious Experience Today*
Mowbray, London, 1990

How firmly do I believe that God loves me
"with a love beyond imagination—
no matter what I did?"

*Let nothing disturb you;
Let nothing dismay you;
All things pass.
God never changes.
Patience attains. / All that it strives for.
He who has God. / Finds he lacks nothing:
God alone suffices.* Saint Teresa's Bookmark

How long I knelt
I don't remember

The LORD spoke to Elijah . . .
"Go out and stand before me
on top of the mountain . . ."
The LORD . . . sent a furious wind . . .
but the LORD was not in the wind. . . .
Then there was an earthquake—
but the LORD was not in the earthquake.
After the earthquake there was a fire—
but the LORD was not in the fire.
And after the fire
there was the soft whisper of a voice.
When Elijah heard it, he covered his face.
1 Kings 19:11–13

One day . . . I walked through the country
past flowering meadows . . .
I stopped, looked around, and up to the sky—
and then I went down on my knees. . . .
How long I knelt there . . .
memory can no longer recall.
But I know that on that day, in that hour,
my new life started.
Viktor Frankl: *Man's Search For Meaning*

When did I feel overwhelmed to the point
that I felt moved to kneel or to pray?

Whenever beauty overwhelms us,
whenever wonder silences
our chattering hopes and worries,
we are close to worship. Richard C. Cabot

Journal

Week 3 — Day four

Journal

Failure opened a window to the Father

*When the face is sad
the heart grows wiser.* Ecclesiastes 7:3

Francis Buckley teaches theology
at the University of San Francisco.
He writes in his book
Growing in the Church: From Birth to Death:
"One of the ways
my students have surprised me
is that they find God in failure more than
in success or beauty.
The death of a parent or relative,
the breakup of a love affair,
the loss of a game or a job
are for them windows of discovery.
They realize that they are not
self-sufficient, not in control of life,
so they look beyond themselves.
They learn a lot from failure. It is one of
the paradoxical secrets of Christian life."

How has adversity helped me to find God?

*Not until each loom is silent
And the shuttles cease to fly,
Will God unroll the pattern
And explain the reason why.
The dark threads are as needful
In the weaver's skillful hand
As the threads of gold and silver
for the pattern which is planned.* Author unknown

A deep peace came over me

*You, LORD, give perfect peace
to those who keep their purpose firm
and put their trust in you.* Isaiah 26:3

A young woman was a secretary
to an executive in the entertainment field.
Fed up with what she saw around her,
she went to a park one evening.
She writes:
"I walked through the park and
sat down by the water intending to read. . . .
Quite suddenly,
I felt lifted beyond all the turmoil. . . .
The disillusionment and cynicism
were gone and I felt compassion . . .
for all the people in the world.
I was possessed by a peace
that I never felt before or since . . .
I felt it was an experience of God."
David Hay: *Religious Experience Today*, Mowbray 1990

As a result of her experience,
the young woman left her job and embarked
on a ministry in social work—
something that brought her great peace.

What restores my strength and peace of mind when I get fed up with things?

*Great lives never go out.
They go on.* Benjamin Harrison

Week 3

Day six

Journal

Because of how I felt, I put it back

Praise the LORD, my soul! . . .
You have made so many things!
How wisely you made them all! . . .
Praise the LORD, my soul! Psalms 104:1, 24, 35

A high school student wrote:
"I was lying on some grass fishing.
I'd picked a secluded spot and was all alone.
Suddenly, I found myself listening to sounds
and looking at nature around me.
I felt so good. I think it was the first time
I took nature for what it is—beautiful!
I sat up and felt happy just to be alive.
I loved everything: the trees, the grass.
Then I hooked a fish.
It was the biggest one I'd caught all day.
But then I did something I hadn't planned.
Because of the way I felt, I put the fish
back into the water and let it swim away." Anonymous

Can I recall a time when I was seized
suddenly and unexpectedly
by the beauty of God's creation?
When? Where? With what results?

Out of the vast comes the nearness;
For the God whose love we sing
Lends a little bit of his heaven
to every living thing.
Augustus Wright Bornberger

We could hardly speak for joy

Every good gift . . . comes from heaven.
James 1:17

Ardis Whitman
and her husband were enroute
to Nova Scotia for a much-needed vacation.
Dark, stormy-looking clouds filled the sky.
They were hoping to reach a restaurant
before rain came. Suddenly, the sky fell in.
Driving was impossible. Ardis writes:
"We pulled off
onto the shoulder of the road and stopped.
Then, as though someone had turned off
a celestial faucet, it ended.
A thin radiance, like a spark of gold,
spread out from the clouds,
catching the tops of trees.
Every blade of grass was crystalline
as the sun flashed on trembling drops.
The very road shone.
We could hardly speak for awe and joy. . .
Suddenly we know who we are
and what we are meant to be."
Reader's Digest, April 1965, "Overtaken by Joy"

How do I interpret the final comment?
What point is she making?

*Moments of joy are proof
that at the heart of darkness
an unquenchable light shines.* Ardis Whitman

Journal

Week 4: *Word of the Father*

Love Story

The film *Laura* concerns a young woman
who is shot in her apartment.
A young detective named Mark MacPherson
is assigned to the case and spends hours
searching the apartment for clues.
He even reads her letters and her diary.

Then something strange happens.
From what Mark learns about Laura,
especially from her letters and diary,
he finds himself falling in love with her—
even though he has never met her.

Late one night
Mark is seated in Laura's apartment
pondering the case. He falls asleep. Suddenly
a sound awakens him. He looks up.

Standing in the doorway
is a beautiful woman. It's Laura.
Mark can hardly believe his eyes.

Then the story unfolds.
Laura had gone off for a weekend of quiet—
away from TV, radio, and newspapers.
She returned unaware of what had happened.

It turns out that the victim—
whose face was disfigured in the slaying—
was not Laura, but an acquaintance
who asked to use her apartment
during her absence.

The film ends
with Laura and Mark falling in love,
marrying, and living happily ever after.

That story
is a kind of parable of God and ourselves.

Like Mark,
who found himself in Laura's apartment,
we find ourselves in God's "apartment:"
the universe.

And like Mark, who fell in love with Laura
by studying her apartment,
so we fall in love with God,
by studying his "apartment."

Hopefully, our story will end
as Mark's did—
with us falling in love with "our Father"
and living happily with him forever after.

This week's meditations
focus on the "love story" between
our Father and ourselves.

The love story begins with creation

*In the beginning,
when God created the universe,
the earth was formless and desolate . . .
and the Spirit of God was moving
over the water. Then God commanded,
"Let there be light."* Genesis 1:1–3

Four days before Christmas 1968,
Apollo 8 lifted off with astronauts
Borman, Anders, and Lovell aboard.
On Christmas Eve, all contact with *Apollo 8*
was lost as it disappeared behind the moon.
Millions of people sat glued to TV sets,
waiting and praying for its safety.
Then came a spectacular moment.
As *Apollo 8* reappeared and came into view,
the crew took turns
reading the biblical story of creation.
It portrays God creating everything
in an orderly way over a six-day period,
much as an artisan works.
The point of this quaint imagery is to teach
that creation did not occur by chance.
It was the loving act of a loving God.

What did God see in us that made him
create us and share his love with us?

*God does not love us for what we are,
but we are because God loves us.*
Peter van Breeman

Journal

Week 4

Day two

Journal

We are created in God's image

*God took some soil from the ground
and formed a man out of it;
he breathed life-giving breath into
his nostrils. . . . Then the LORD God . . .
took out one of the man's ribs and . . .
formed a woman.* Genesis 2:7, 21–22

The high point of creation
is the fashioning of the first human beings.
The Bible portrays it with quaint, warm,
and moving imagery:
The purpose of this imagery is to reveal
the intimacy between God and human beings.
It shows God sharing with them
a part of his own life and being.
To appreciate
how revolutionary this idea was,
recall that the biblical creation story
was penned at a time when other religions
were stressing the distance between
gods and humans.
The bible stresses their nearness.
God's love is deeper and closer
than the love of parents for their child.

How deeply do I believe in God's love for me?

*God says, "Can a woman forget her own baby
and not love the child she bore?
Even if a mother should forget her child,
I will never forget you."* Isaiah 49:15

God upholds and sustains us

Paul writes:
"God is actually not far
from any one of us. . . .
"In God we live and move and exist."
Acts 17:27–28

Think of creation
as being like images on a movie screen.
Think of the Father
as being like the projector,
that put and keeps the images on the screen.
Just as the images on the screen
would cease to exist if the projector
withdrew its light from them,
so creation would cease to exist
if the Father withdrew his power from it.
Furthermore,
as the projector's light in the images
gives it a true *presence* on the screen,
so the Father's sustaining action in us
gives him a true *presence* in our world.

How aware am I of my dependence
on the Father for giving me life
and sustaining me in life?
How can I become more appreciative of it?

Earthly props are useless,
On Thy grace I fall;
Earthly strength is weakness,
Father, on Thee I call. John Oxenham

Journal

Week 4 — Day four

Journal

The Father speaks three words

*God spoke to our ancestors . . .
through the prophets,
but in these last days
God has spoken to us through his Son.* Hebrews 1:1–2

The Father
has revealed himself through "three words."
The "first word" is his "cosmic" word.
As a song reveals something of its writer,
creation reveals something of its creator.
Saint Paul explains it this way:
"Since God created the world,
his invisible qualities . . . are perceived
in the things God has made." Romans 1:20
God's "second word"
is the "inspired" word of scripture.
God spoke it, mainly, by deeds, not words.
That is, God didn't say, "Israel, I love you."
God showed his love by loving actions.
Finally, the Father spoke his "third word."
It is called the "incarnate" word.
We give it this name
because God spoke it through his Son Jesus.
Jesus is the "word of God made flesh."

Which of God's "three words"
speaks to me most eloquently? Why?

It is visible that *God is,*
it is invisible what *God is.* Stephen Charnock

The Father speaks the cosmic word

O LORD, my God, how great you are!
You are clothed in majesty and glory . . .
You use the clouds as your chariot and
ride on the wings of the wind. Psalms 104:1–3

Someone wrote,
"When I behold the cosmos,
there dawns in my consciousness
a faint glimmer of what God must be like.
For the Creator has left his 'signature'
on all of creation—planets, stars, people.
Just as a song gives me a tiny glimmer
of a songwriter's personality,
and just as a house's furnishings give me
a tiny glimmer of its owner's personality,
so the cosmos gives me a tiny glimmer
of what my Father must be like.
It is, in this sense, that the cosmos
is my Father's 'cosmic word' to me."

O LORD . . . your greatness is seen
in all the world! . . . What am I,
that you think of me? (Psalms 8:1,4 adapted)
How do I answer this question?

Nature has perfections
in order to show
that she is the image of God;
and defects to show
that she is only God's image.
Blaise Pascal

Journal

Week 4

Day six

Journal

The Father speaks the inspired word

What does the scripture say? Galatians 4:30

The beauty of the cosmos gives us
a tiny glimmer of what the Father is like.
But that is all it gives: a tiny glimmer.
This is because
reasoning from the beauty of the cosmos
to the beauty of God can take us only so far.
It can't bridge the entire gap and
reveal everything about the Father.
*If reason enabled me
to know everything about God,
God would not have to reveal himself. . . .
Reason alone can't bridge
from an infinite supreme being . . .
to a caring being.*
Mortimer Adler: Interview with Bill Moyers
This gap can be bridged only by
God's self-revelation through the Bible.
And so we must turn to the Bible
for a better picture of God.

How are the Old Testament and the New Testament similar, but also different?

*Radio is like the Old Testament;
you hear God's Word;
TV is like the New Testament;
you not only hear God's Word
but also see it come alive in Jesus.*
Fulton Sheen (adapted)

The Father speaks the incarnate word

*Philip said to Jesus,
"L%%ORD%% show us the Father." . . .
Jesus answered . . .
"Whoever has seen me has seen the Father."*
John 14:8–9

A word welcomes, invites, and reveals.
Jesus is the "Word of God"
because he reveals the Father.
He is the "Word of God" become flesh.
Jesus reveals the Father
not only by what he says,
but also by what he does—and is.
St. Paul called Jesus "the exact likeness
of God's own being." Hebrews 1:3
But Jesus is the "Word of God"
in still another way.
Jesus reveals me to myself.
Jesus is the perfect image
of what I should strive to be.
He is the perfect image
of imperfect humanity.
And so Jesus is the "Word of God"
because he reveals to me who God is,
who I am, and what I can become,
if I open myself to the Holy Spirit.

What keeps me from "hearing" Jesus better?

*To be ignorant of the Scriptures
is to be ignorant of Christ.* Saint Jerome

Journal

Week 5 — *Word of the Father*

Cosmic Word

Late one afternoon,
archaeologist Gene Savoy became lost
in a Peruvian jungle.
He searched and searched for the tiny trail
that had led him into the jungle.
But he couldn't find it.

In a state of panic and near exhaustion,
he stopped dead.
Then a strange thought flashed
across his mind:
God is in this jungle. It is God's house.

Gene had been first introduced to
the beauties of nature when he was a boy
in Oregon. His parents had taught him
that God had created the universe,
sustains it, and resides in it.

Why had he closed his eyes
to God's presence in the jungles of Peru?
Didn't God create them, also?
Doesn't God reside in them, also?

Instantly, Gene relaxed
and put all his trust in God,
in whose house he was. He said later:

*I looked up
into the beautiful emerald world
of wild orchids and fragrant blossoms
where hummingbirds hovered.*

*Yes, God was here, too.
My heart quieted.*

At that moment something within Gene
seemed to say, "Walk to the left."
He did.
And there was the tiny trail for which
he had been searching so frantically.

Last week we saw
how the Father revealed himself to us
through three words:

— the cosmic word (creation),
— the inspired word (scripture), and
— the incarnate word (Jesus).

In the weeks ahead,
we will focus on each of these three words.
This week we begin with the "cosmic word:"
the Father's revelation of himself
through his marvelous creation.

In other words, as a song or a painting
says something of its creator,
so the cosmos says something of God.
Saint Paul puts it this way:

*Since God created the world,
his invisible qualities . . . are perceived
in the things God has made.* Romans 1:20

God said, 'Let there be light.'

In the beginning . . . God commanded, "Let lights appear in the sky to separate day from night." Genesis 1:1, 14, 17

The surface temperature of the sun
is 12,000 degrees Fahrenheit—
just enough to warm planet Earth,
but not too much.
The moon causes the tides on Earth.
If the moon were only 50,000 miles away
instead of 240,000, tides would be so great
they would flood every continent on Earth.
Earth tilts 23-degrees.
If it weren't tilted just the right amount,
ocean vapors would flow north and south
and bury every continent under tons of ice.
Finally, if Earth's atmosphere
were much thinner, millions of meteors
would fail to burn up falling through space,
and would come crashing down on us.

What is my reaction as I contemplate
the marvelous structure of the universe?

*The sun is so large that, if it were hollow,
it could contain more than one million
worlds of the size of our Earth.
There are stars in space so large
that they could easily hold
500 million suns of the size of ours.*
Morris Mandell

Journal

Week 5 Day two

Journal

God said, 'Let the earth produce plants.'

*The earth produced all kinds of plants,
and God was pleased with what he saw.
Evening passed and morning came—
that was the third day.* Genesis 1:12

Decades ago, a new species of cactus
was introduced into Australia.
It was supposed to serve
as a kind of natural "fence."
Then came the bad news.
The cactus had no native Australian insects
to control its growth. Result?
It ran wild and, eventually, blanketed
an area about the size of England.
The invading cactus drove people not only
off their farms, but out of their villages.
Entomologists finally found and imported
an insect that fed exclusively off the cactus.
Today, the cactus has retreated into
a small area, and provides just enough food
for the right number of insects to control it.

What is my reaction as I contemplate
the marvelous checks and balances
that protect our cosmos and our planet?

*We die on the day
when our lives cease to be illumined
by the steady radiance, renewed daily,
of a wonder, the source of which
is beyond reason.* Dag Hammarskjold

Day three — Week 5

God said, 'Let birds fill the air.'

Journal

*God created . . . all kinds of birds.
He blessed them all and . . .
told the birds to increase in number.*
Genesis 1:21–22

Over 8,000 known species of birds
fly across the face of our Earth daily.
Many of these are migratory birds
that navigate with pinpoint accuracy.
Some scientists suggest that they use
the sun and stars as compass points.
Take the Manx Shearwater birds.
One of them was captured from its burrow
on the coast of Wales, banded, and flown
over three thousand miles to Boston.
There it was released.
Within two weeks, it was back in Wales.
More amazing,
it was back in the same burrow
from which it was captured.

How would a small bird, feed, sleep, rest
during such a long journey?

*Job said to Zophar,
"Even the birds and animals
have much they could teach you;
ask the creatures of earth and sea
for their wisdom. All of them know
that the LORD's hand made them."*
Job 12:7–9

Week 5 — Day four

Journal

God said, 'Let us make human beings.'

So God created human beings, making them to be like himself. Genesis 1:26

Whittaker Chambers was a U.S. Communist, who broke with the party in the mid-1900s. He dates his break from a casual happening. He says:
"I was watching my daughter eat. . . .
I liked to watch her
even when she smeared porridge on her face
or dropped it meditatively on the floor.
My eye came to rest on
the delicate convolutions of her ear . . .
The thought passed through my mind . . .
'Those ears were not created
by any chance coming together of atoms' . . .
The thought was involuntary . . .
I had to crowd it out of my mind.
If I had completed it, I should've had to say:
'Design presupposes God.' . . .
At that moment, the finger of God was laid on my forehead." *Witness,* Random House 1952, p. 16

When did I feel God's finger on my forehead?

*God in heaven, when the idea of you
awakes in my heart, let it not be like
a frightened bird thrashing about in panic,
but like a child waking from a nap—
its face aglow with a smile.*
Soren Kierkegaard (free translation)

And so the cosmos was completed

I will praise you, LORD, with all my heart.
I will tell of all the wonderful things
you have done. Psalms 9:1

In his book *Makes Me Wanna Holler,*
Nathan McCall describes the impact
that meditation had upon him
during his confinement in prison.
He writes:
"I'd get these grinding migraines . . .
I'd stretch out on my bunk . . .
and go into deep meditation. . . .
I'd concentrate hard and command
every one of my body parts to chill. . . .
Then I'd take my imagination
and soar from the prison yard . . .
I'd venture beyond the earth
and wander through the galaxy, pondering
the vastness of what God has done. . . .
When the concentration was really good,
I'd lose all feeling in my body,
and . . . feel at one with the universe."
Makes Me Wanna Holler, Vintage Books

How greatly does meditation on creation
affect my faith or my appreciation of God?

One cannot help but be in awe
when he contemplates the mysteries . . .
of the marvelous structure of reality.
Albert Einstein

Journal

Week 5 — Day six

Journal

Lord, your glory is seen everywhere

*When I look at the sky
which you have made,
at the moon and the stars
which you have set in their places—
what are human beings,
that you think of them;
mere mortals that you care for them?*
Psalms 8: 3–4

Has not everyone, at one time in life,
climbed a hill and gazed at the sky above
and the fields below—and asked,
"Whence all of this? Who put it here?"
Why the newborn calf staggering alongside
its mother grazing in the meadow?
Why the thousands of daisies
dancing daintily along the fence row?
Why the summer sun
ripening these groves of fruit trees?
Why these acres clothed in beauty?
Why this world of birth, growing, and dying?
Does it speak to the secret
of my own graced existence?

How might I answer these questions?

*Scattering a thousand graces,
he passed through these groves in haste,
and looking upon them as he went,
left them by his glance alone,
clothed in beauty.* Saint John of the Cross

Praise the Lord, all you creatures!

Praise the LORD . . . with trumpets. . . .
Praise him with drums and dancing. . . .
Praise him with harps and flutes. . . .
Psalms 150:1, 3, 4, 6

An old legend says
that after God created human beings
he summoned the angels and asked,
"Is there anything more I might make?"
The angels caucused together.
Then Gabriel said: "Lord, we'd like you
to give the things you created
a way to thank you for making them.
God sat down and thought and thought.
Suddenly, God jumped up and said,
"Let there be music!"
With that, every bird began to warble.
Every brook began to babble.
Every breeze began to sing, and
every tree began to sway and clap its hands.
When the human beings saw this,
they couldn't help but join in.
And that's how music came to be.

To what extent do I agree that
"To sing is to pray twice"?

Music expresses
that which cannot be said in words
and about which
it is impossible to be silent. Victor Hugo

Journal

Week 6 — *Word of the Father*

Cosmos & scientists

Scientists surmise that eons ago
something like a bomb was poised in space.
It exploded, and its contents flew outward,
gradually forming our universe.

Centuries ago, Saint Augustine suggested that
God could have created a "seed"
from which our cosmos slowly emerged.

Astronomer Carl Sagan
estimated that it took 15 million years
for the cosmos to reach its present state.
He said that if this 15-million-year period
were telescoped into one year,
the cosmic timetable would look this:

January 1	The "Big Bang" takes place
May 1	Milky Way Galaxy appears
December 31	Humans appear (11:30 p.m.)
December 31	Jesus appears (11:59 p.m.)
January 1	Space Age begins

In September 1975,
the Associated Press broke the news
that astronomers had picked up
microwave signals of the "big bang."
British astronomer Sir Bernard Lovell
said that they were detected accidentally
while testing
space communication equipment.

Later, the signals were monitored by
a rocket shot above the earth's atmosphere.

Robert Jastrow, former director of NASA's
Goddard Institute for Space Studies,
said in an interview with Bill Durbin:

*Astronomers now find they have painted
themselves into a corner, because
they have proven, by their own methods,
that the world began abruptly
in an act of creation to which
you can trace the seeds of every star,
every planet, every living thing in
this cosmos and on the earth.*
"Christianity Today" Aug. 6, 1982

Jastrow concludes,

*For the scientist who has lived
by his faith in the power of reason,
the story ends like a bad dream.
He has scaled the mountains of ignorance;
he is about to conquer the highest peak;
as he pulls himself over the final rock,
he is greeted by a band of theologians
who have been sitting there for centuries.*
"The New York Times Magazine," June 25, 1978

This week's meditations
focus on the reflections of scientists
as they explore the mysteries of our cosmos.

The cosmos is beyond imagining

Journal

God made . . . the moon to rule the night.
Genesis 1:16

Millions of people on earth watched on TV
as the moon module, *Eagle*, descended slowly
toward the surface of the moon.
Cheers rang out when Armstrong announced,
"Houston, the Eagle has landed."
The time was July 20, 1969, 4:17 p.m., E.D.T.
Physicist Robert Hofstadler spoke for many
when he said, "In a thousand years
there will be few things remembered,
but this will be one of them."
What journalist William F. Buckley said
after the spacecraft's liftoff from Florida,
applied now.
A reporter asked him, "If you were asked
to describe what you just saw,
how would you do it?"
Buckley said, "With silence!"

Where was I at the time of the moon landing?
What do I think is its main significance?

[The moon landing] symbolized
man's wondrous capacity for questing. . . .
It was also a reminder of something else. . . .
Man inhabits a smallish planet . . .
that occupies the tiniest corner of
a universe that is beyond comprehension.
Time magazine

Week 6

Day two

Journal

Science and religion are sisters

God looked at everything he had made, and he was very pleased. Genesis 1:31

Wernher von Braun has been called
the "20th-century Columbus."
More than any other scientist,
he is responsible for putting us on the moon.
Born in Germany, he surrendered to the Allies
near the end of World War II,
when the Russians marched on Berlin.
He was sent to the United States
and, eventually, became the director
of Alabama's Marshall Space Flight Center.
He said in a lecture:
"The natural laws of the universe
are so precise that we have no difficulty
building a spaceship to fly to the moon, and
we can time the flight with the precision
of a fraction of a second. . . .
Anything . . . so precisely balanced . . .
can only be the product of a Divine Idea."
Unpublished Lecture

Why can't chance explain such precision?
How are science and religion related?

Science and religion are sisters.
Through science we strive to learn
more of the mysteries of creation.
Through religion, we seek to know
the Creator. Wernher von Braun

The Father became closer and closer

I know a certain Christian man who . . . was snatched up to the highest heaven . . . and there he heard things which cannot be put into words. 2 Corinthians 12:2–4

Astronaut James Irwin says that when he, Scott, and Worden, blasted off on Apollo 15 to the moon, he thought it was merely "to get rocks and take some pictures." What happened, however, changed his life. He writes in his book *To Rule the Night:* "I wish I had been a writer or a poet so that I could convey more adequately the feeling of this flight. It has been sort of a slow-breaking revelation for me. The ultimate effect has been to deepen and strengthen all the religious insight I ever had. It has remade my faith." Later, he said in a public lecture: "God became closer and closer to us as we ventured deeper and deeper into space. . . . I felt the power of God as I never felt it before."

When did I feel God's power in my life?

On the moon the total picture of the power of God and His Son Jesus Christ became abundantly clear to me.
James Irwin: To Rule the Night

Journal

Week 6

Day four

Journal

A tiny door has been opened

*All we can do
is guess about the things of earth.
Who, then, can hope to understand
heavenly things.* Wisdom 9:16

Von Braun said: "Manned space flight
is an amazing achievement!
But it has opened for us thus far only
a tiny door for viewing
the awesome reaches of space. . . .
For every new answer,
a dozen new questions spring up.
Science is facing wide-open frontiers
in many fields; the atomic nucleus
is becoming more and more enigmatic;
the origin and structure of the universe
are still shrouded in mystery; and the exact
bodily functions of living organisms
still evade complete understanding.
The Golden Age of Science is still ahead."
Wernher von Braun: Unpublished Lecture

How are science and religion related?

*We should remember that science exists
only because there are people,
and the concept exists
only in the minds of men.
Behind these concepts lies reality—
revealed to us only by the grace of God.*
Wernher von Braun: Unpublished Lecture

Scientists respond in different ways

Jesus said, "This people ... will look and look, but not see."
Matthew 13:14–15

Robert Jastrow is the former director of NASA's Goddard Institute of Space Studies. He taught astronomy at Columbia University and did a series of science programs on CBS. His three books, *Red Giants and White Dwarfs, Until the Sun Dies,* and *The Enchanted Loom* trace the story of the universe from creation to our day. Concerning the response of some scientists to recent findings relating to the universe's origin, he says:
"You might say this would make them more inclined to accept religious views on the origin of the world.
But their ... general response has been ... to avoid the implications."
"Christianity Today" Interview with Bill Durbin

Why should some scientists tend to respond in this fashion?

The scientist behaves the way the rest of us do when our beliefs are in conflict with the evidence. . . . We pretend the conflict does not exist or we paper it over with meaningless phrases. Robert Jastrow

Journal

Week 6 — Day six

Journal

Scientists reason to the unseen

The sky reveals . . . what God has done!
Psalms 19:3–4

One night in 1781, William Herschel
was scanning the sky with his telescope.
Suddenly, he caught sight of a new "star."
It turned out to be a seventh planet, Uranus.
Other astronomers now monitored its orbit.
Soon they noticed something strange.
At one point, Uranus deviated slightly
from its charted course.
In time, a French astronomer, Leverrier,
reasoned that the deviation
had to be caused by the gravitational pull
of another unseen, undiscovered planet.
He calculated where the planet would
have to be to cause this orbital deviation.
But he didn't have a telescope
powerful enough to check the spot
to see if it was actually there.
He contacted a large observatory in Berlin
and told them where to look.
There they found an eighth planet—Neptune.

How does the science of astronomy
show us how to reason something
that our senses cannot perceive directly?

*I found him in the shining of the stars,
I marked him in the flowering of his fields.*
Alfred Lord Tennyson

Scientists have a real advantage

God's invisible qualities . . . are perceived in the things that God has made. Romans 1:20

Warren Weaver says
scientists have a real advantage
in conceiving and believing in God. Reason?
They deal with the undefinable.
For example,
no scientist has ever seen an "electron."
It is simply the name scientists give
to a consistent set of things
that happen in certain circumstances.
Sometimes the electron behaves
like a particle; sometimes, like a wave.
Weaver says:
"All this may seem ridiculous to you.
But just as there are various complex ideas
about the electron—
it is sometimes one thing, sometimes
another, it can't be seen and can't be
precisely located—
so there are various ideas about God.
He, too, I think, can be neither seen
nor precisely located."
"Can a Scientist Believe in God?" *Redbook,* 12/1967

How do physicists go beyond astronomers
in showing how reason can lead us to God?

Like scripture, nature reveals God.
Anonymous

Journal

Cosmos & religion

Dr. Charles Townes won the Nobel Prize
for his work on the laser.
A major insight into the laser
came while he was sitting on a park bench
looking at flowers. He writes:

Science and religion are very similar.
If we compare how
great scientific ideas arrive, they look
remarkably like religious revelation
viewed in a non-mystical way.

The great scientific discoveries,
the real leaps, do not usually come
from the so-called scientific method
but by revelations which are just as real.
Think magazine

Dr. Wernher von Braun
echoed this very same idea, saying,

While science is not religion,
it is religious activity by its suppositions,
its method of working and
its search for truth.

Albert Einstein took an even bolder step
in relating science to religion, saying:

Science without religion is lame,
religion without science in blind.

All of this represents
somewhat of a revolution in attitude
on the part of many scientists.

Loren Eiseley,
one of our century's foremost interpreters
of evolutionists,
alludes to this attitudinal revolution
in his autobiography *All the Strange Hours*.

Commenting on the section
in Eiseley's autobiography entitled
"Days of the Doubter," Morton Kelsey says,

Eiseley's doubt was not concerning
religion or religious ideas,
but rather doubt in regard to the dogmatism
of the scientific world.
In describing it he shows a new and
increasing openness to [religious ideas].

Kelsey concludes:

There has been a scientific revolution
in our century.
More and more evidence has accumulated
that the materialistic view of the universe
is not adequate.
It simply does not take all the facts
into account.   Afterlife, Paulist Press, 1979

This week's meditations
focus on the changing stance
of many scientists to religion.

I had to reopen my mind to God

*Turn back and serve God with
ten times more determination.*
Baruch 4:28

Britain's Jane Goodall
is an expert on wildlife and conservation.
She has lectured at Yale University,
written for the *New York Times,* and
appeared on such TV shows as "Nightline,"
"20/20," and "Good Morning America."
In a moment of candor, she confessed:
"When I left home
and faced the realities of the world,
I put my thoughts of God
in cold storage for a while, because
I couldn't reconcile
what I believed, deep inside,
with what was going on around me.
But that early period
when God was as real as the wind . . .
left me an inner peace,
which as I grew older,
swelled—until, perforce,
I had to open my mind to God again."

*With peace in the soul,
we can face the very worst experience.
Without peace in the soul,
we can't even face the simple task
of writing a letter.*
Anonymous British psychiatrist (adapted)

Journal

Week 7

Day two

Journal

Science & religion are complementary

*Jesus said, "Your light must shine
before people, so that they will . . .
praise your Father in heaven."* Matthew 5:16

Nobel prize winner Max Planck formulated
the quantum theory and fueled the
quantum-relativistic revolution in physics.
He writes:
"There can never be any real opposition
between religion and science;
for one is the complement of the other.
Every serious and reflective person realizes,
I think, that the religious element in nature
must be recognized and cultivated
if all the powers of the human soul
are to act together
in perfect balance and harmony. . . .
It was not by any accident
that the greatest thinkers of all ages
were also deeply religious souls,
even though they made no public show
of their religious feeling." *Where is Science Going?*

Why do famous people
shy from a public witness to their faith?
To what extent
should they witness to their faith in God?

*A little science and faith is far;
A lot of science and faith is near.*
Anonymous

He watched a girl be healed by prayer

I do have faith, but not enough.
Help me have more. Mark 9:24

Alexis Carrel was a Nobel prize winner
and an unbelieving French surgeon.
Then, at the shrine in Lourdes, France,
he saw a girl healed before his very eyes.
He was stunned, unable to think.
Later, he and two other doctors examined
the girl and agreed she was totally healed.
But he still had "intellectual doubts."
That night he went for a long walk to think
things out. Later, he wrote (in the third
person) in his book *The Voyage to Lourdes:*
"Back in the hotel . . .
he took the big green notebook from his bag
and sat down to write his observations. . . .
It was now three o'clock. . . .
A new coolness penetrated the open window.
He felt the serenity of nature enter his soul.
All intellectual doubts vanished."
Carrel went on to become a deeply
committed Christian the rest of his life.

Why would it be so hard for a scientist
to accept Jesus' invitation to believe?

A miracle . . . strengthens faith.
But faith in God is less apt to proceed from
miracles than miracles from faith in God.
Frederick Buechner

Journal

Week 7 — Day four

Journal

Prayer is good medicine

Jesus healed many. Mark 1:34

Dr. Larry Dossey
wrote a bestseller called *Healing Words.*
His sequel book, *Prayer is Good Medicine,*
is a kind of manual for integrating prayer
into the healing process.
Dossey begins by noting that medicine
is now taking prayer much more seriously.
For example,
medical journals are soliciting articles
on the healing effects of prayer.
The prestigious Harvard Medical School
hosted a conference entitled
"Spirituality and Healing in Medicine."
Finally, medical schools are offering
courses on alternative medicine.
Many of these courses
stress spiritual issues in health care,
especially the role of prayer.

How do I account for the growing interest in
the role of prayer in the healing process?

*The Templeton Foundation recently awarded
"faith and medicine" grants
to Johns Hopkins School of Medicine
and four other schools. . . .
Ten years ago,
this would have been unheard of.*
The Tampa Tribune

Day five Week 7

The power of prayer is demonstrable

Journal

*Jesus made the disciples get into the boat
and go on ahead to the other side
of the lake, while he sent the people away.
After sending the people away,
he went to a hill by himself to pray.*
Matthew 14:22–23

Nobel Prize winner Dr. Alexis Carrell
wrote a book called *Man the Unknown.*
In it, he makes this striking statement:
"Prayer is the most powerful form
of energy we can generate. . . .
The influence of prayer
on the human mind and body is
as demonstrable as secreting glands. . . .
Only in prayer do we achieve
that complete and harmonious assembly
of body, mind, and spirit
which gives the frail human reed
its unshakable strength."

What is one effect
that regular prayer has had on my life?
What keeps me from sharing my conviction
about prayer's power with others?

*When we pray we link ourselves
to the inexhaustible motive power
which spins the universe.
We ask that a part of this power
be apportioned to our needs.* Alexis Carrel

Week 7 — Day six

Journal

Mind and my heart point to God

Can you guide the stars season by season?
Job 38:32

A. Cressy Morrison cites the following experiment as a mathematical exercise that points to a Creator. Mark 10 coins "1" to "10," put them in your pocket, and give them a good shake. Now try to draw them out in sequence from "1" to "10," putting each coin back after each withdrawal. Your chances of drawing "1" is one in ten. Your chances of drawing "1" and "2" in succession is one in a hundred. Your chances of drawing "1," "2," and "3" in succession is one in a thousand. This continues until your chances of drawing "1" through "10" in succession "skyrocket" to the unbelievable figure of one in 10 billion. *Man Does Not Stand Alone*

What is Morrison's point?

When the proofs, the figures, were ranged in columns before me . . . How soon unaccountably I became tired and sick. Till rising and gliding out I wander'd off by myself In the mystical moist night air, and from time to time Looked up in perfect silence at the stars.
Walt Whitman: "When I Heard the Learn'd Astronomer"

Science and religion go hand-in-hand

Journal

*If the LORD does not build the house,
the work of the builders is useless.*
Psalms 127:1

"[The future of the human family]
must always form the chief interest
of all technical endeavors.
Never forget this in the midst
of your diagrams and equations."
Albert Einstein

"More and more of the decisions
which affect human lives
will be scientific decisions.
They must not be made by persons
who are not equipped
to understand the moral consequences."
Dr. Aaron Ihde

What does Dr. Ihde mean when he says
that scientific decisions must be made
by persons who are equipped to understand
the moral consequences?

*Our scientific power
has outrun our spiritual power.
We have guided missiles and misguided men.
Science investigates; religion interprets.
Science gives man knowledge
which is power;
religion gives man wisdom
which is control.*
Martin Luther King, Jr. *Strength To Love*

Week 8 — *Word of the Father*

Inspired word

Daniel Harrington is a biblical scholar.
When asked where he finds God, he said:

"I stutter. . . .
As a young boy I read in a newspaper
that Moses stuttered.
I looked it up in the Bible, and sure enough
in Exodus 4:10, Moses says to God:
'I am slow of speech and slow of tongue.'"

But Harrington found much more than this.
He found the story of God's self-revelation
to Moses and of God's commissioning of Moses
to speak that self-revelation to the world.
Harrington ended, "I found God in the Bible,
and I have continued to do so ever since."
Then he added this caution:

The encounter with God through the Bible
cannot be programmed or forced. . . .
God takes the initiative in this relationship
and leads us where he wants us to go.
James Martin: "How Can I Find God? Another Look,"
America magazine, August 30, 1997

An example will illustrate.
Two young men were canoeing on a river
in the Canadian wilds.
One day they both became ill.
Fortunately, they spotted a trapper's cabin.
They beached their canoe
and walked up to the cabin.

It was unlocked.
In one corner was a cot.
On it lay an open Bible with a note.
It read:

Your cabin saved my life.
I was seriously ill and needed shelter.
Your cabin provided it.
I have no money with which to repay you.
I can only promise you God's blessing.
Read the passage from Matthew 25
directly beneath his note.

The passage reads:

"Come and possess the kingdom
which has been prepared for you . . .
I was a stranger and you received me . . .
I was sick and you took care of me . . .
Whenever you did this for one of the least
important of these followers of mine,
you did it for me."

Later, one of the young men said,
"I'd read that passage many times,
but I never really understood it
until that day."

This week's meditations focus on
the "inspired word" of Scripture
and how our heavenly Father continues
to speak to us through it.

I found the Bible to be fantastic

Jesus said, "These very Scriptures speak about me." John 5:39

Paul Stookey was in the singing group
"Peter, Paul, and Mary;" but not happy.
One day he told singer Bob Dylan about it.
Dylan told him to read the Bible.
Stookey said later:
"I started reading the New Testament. . . .
All the truths I sought were contained
in the life of this man. It was fantastic . . .
but it never occurred to me
that he could really be the Son of God."
Then one night a young man came backstage
in Austin, Texas, and talked with him
about Jesus. Stookey said:
"This guy made all the reading
in the Scriptures make sense. . . .
So, wow, I started to pray with him,
and I asked Jesus to come in
and take over my life." And he did.
Bob Combs and Scott Ross: *"Peter, me, and Mary"*
Campus Life, May 1972
Stookey still had a long way to go;
but his spiritual journey was begun.

How content am I with my life right now?

*The Good News can be heard
far more distinctly with your heart
than with your ears.* Anonymous

Journal

Week 8 — Day two

Journal

As I read the Bible, Jesus became real

The word of God is alive and active. . . .
It cuts all the way through, to where
the soul and spirit meet. Hebrews 4:12

Margaret Mehren was a member
of the Nazi youth movement in Germany.
After the war, she learned of the atrocities
in Nazi death camps and was shocked.
She vowed never again to believe an adult.
It was in this frame of mind
that she began to question her own atheism.
One day she happened upon a Bible.
Out of curiosity, she began to read it.
But it made no sense at all. She put it down.
Then one night she picked it up again.
This time it opened to the Gospels.
Then something remarkable happened.
She wrote later:
"When I read the words of Jesus . . .
I knew he was there [in the room with me,]
even though I could not hear or see anything.
Jesus was real, more real than anything
around me. . . . I was no longer alone.
My life was no longer a dead-end street."

When did Jesus start to become real for me?

Amazing grace! how sweet the sound
That saved a wretch like me. . . .
How precious did the grace appear
The hour I first believed. John Newton

As I read the Bible, peace came over me

The word of God . . .
judges the desires and thoughts
of the heart. Hebrews 4:12

Charlie Pitts built the Toronto subway.
As his business prospered,
he and his wife began to drift apart.
One day, she went to their home in Miami.
There, as a kind of last resort,
she began reading the Bible.
A feeling of peace came over her.
She called Charlie and asked him to come.
When she told him what had happened,
he looked at her in disbelief.
But after watching her closely for days,
he knew that her newfound faith was real.
They began reading the Bible together.
To make a long story short,
that was the start of a new life for both.
Reported by Billy Graham
in "What the Bible Says to Me" *Readers Digest,* 5/1969

How convinced am I
that God's grace and power can do for me
what it did for Charlie Pitts and his wife?

When you go to pray to me,
I will listen to you.
When you look for me,
you will find me.
Jeremiah 29:12–13 NAB

Journal

Week 8 — Day four

Journal

As I read the Bible, God found me

*Everything written in the Scriptures . . .
was written . . .
that we might have hope.* Romans 15:4

German theologian Jurgen Multmann
was a POW during World War II.
When he was shown photographs
of piles of naked victims executed
by the Nazis at Belsen and Auschwitz,
his feelings for Germany collapsed.
Then one day he was given a Bible.
These words of Psalm 39
described the inner state of his being:
"I was dumb with silence . . .
and my sorrow was stirred. . . .
Hear my prayer, O Lord . . .
for I am a stranger with thee."
Multman said,
"They were the words of my own heart and
they called my soul to God." He continued,
"Then I came to the story of the passion.
When I read Jesus' death cry,
'My God, why have you forsaken me?' . . .
God found me in the dark pit of my soul."
"Wrestling with God: A meditation" *Christian Century*,
August 13–20, 1997

How do I interpret the last sentence?

*God weeps with us so that one day
we may laugh with God.* Jurgen Moltmann

Day five — Week 8

The Bible changed my life

To God be glory forever! Romans 11:36

William Cowper's life
was filled with mental turmoil and pain.
During a long stay in a mental hospital,
he began reading the Bible and
underwent a genuine conversion.
He turned to writing hymns. Here's one:
"God moves in a mysterious way
His wonders to perform;
He plants His footsteps in the sea
and rides upon the storm.//
You fearful saints, fresh courage take:
The clouds you so much dread
are big with mercy, and
shall break in blessings on your head.//
Judge not the Lord by feeble sense,
but trust Him for His grace;
behind a frowning providence
faith sees a smiling face.//
Blind unbelief is sure to err
and scan His work in vain;
God is His own interpreter,
and He will make it plain."

Which of these images can I relate to best?

When I stand before the throne,
dressed in beauty not my own . . .
Then, Lord, shall I know—not till then—
how much I owe. Anonymous

Journal

Week 8 — Day six

Journal

We must ponder the Bible seriously

*Jesus explained to them
what was said about himself
in all the Scriptures,
beginning with the books of Moses
and the writings of the prophets.* Luke 24:27

Sometimes,
on dark nights or overcast days,
Native Americans became confused
about the direction they were traveling.
So they would walk over to a tree
to see on which side
the branches were better developed
and most parallel to the ground.
This indicated the side of the tree
that was exposed to the longest period
of sunlight and, therefore,
indicated the south side of the tree.
As Native Americans studied trees
to keep from losing their way,
we need to study Scripture to keep from
losing our way as we journey to God.

What keeps me from studying Scripture
and applying its message to my life?

*If you Christians
in India, in Britain, or in America
were like your Bible,
you would conquer India in five years.*
Indian Brahman to a missionary

The Bible is the Father's saving word

*The people . . . listened to the message
with great eagerness, and every day
they studied the Scriptures.*
Acts 17:11

In his *Journal of a Soul,*
John XXIII describes an experience he had
during a retreat in Turkey.
He writes:
"Every evening from the window . . .
I see an assemblage of boats on the Bosporus;
they come round from the Golden Horn
in tens and hundreds . . . a most impressive
spectacle of color and lights.
These lights glow all night
and one can hear the cheerful voices
of the fishermen. . . .
The other night towards one o'clock,
it was pouring with rain,
but the fishermen were still there. . . .
What a vision of work, zeal, and labor. . . .
We must do as the fishermen of the
Bosporus do." Geoffrey Chapman Ltd. 1965, p. 234

To what extent do I labor more zealously
at succeeding in material undertakings
than I do at succeeding in spiritual ones?

*I have complete confidence in the gospel;
it is God's power to save all who believe.*
Romans 1:16

Journal

Week 9 — *Word of the Father*

Incarnate word

Rabbi David Wolpe explains that for Jews,
Hanukkah celebrates the search for God
in a world that was hostile to that search.

Similarly, he explains that for Christians,
Christmas celebrates the coming of God
in a world that was hostile to that coming.

Thus, Hanukkah and Christmas
are very different holidays.
But both are deeply God-centered and
celebrate the mystery of the Father's love
for the human family.
Both affirm that a loving Father is at the
heart of the Judeo-Christian faith.

And for Christians,
nowhere is the Father's love
more clearly manifested
than in the unfathomable mystery
that the Father sent us his only Son
to be our savior. John 3:16

And so it is to Jesus,
that we must turn to learn about
the Father's love for us and
the Father's plan for us.

Concerning Jesus himself
the Letter to the Hebrews says:

*Jesus reflects
the brightness of God's glory and
is the exact likeness of God's being.*
Hebrews 1:3

The Gospel of John calls Jesus
the "incarnate word" of the Father:
It explains:

*From the very beginning
the Word already existed. . . .
The Word became a human being,
and . . . lived among us.* John 1:1, 14

Jesus said of himself:

*Whoever
has seen me has seen the Father . . .
I am in the Father
and the Father is in me.* John 14:9–10

This week's meditations focus on Jesus,
the "incarnate word" of the Father.
Specifically, they focus on
the Father's love for us and
the Father's plan for us.

Day one Week 9

Love is God's shadow in our universe

Journal

Jesus said,
"Those who love me will obey my teaching.
My Father will love them, and
my Father and I will come to them and
live with them. Those who do not love me
do not obey my teaching." John 14:23–24

The Taj Mahal is located on the Junna River,
125 miles southeast of Delhi India.
It was built in the 17th century
by Emperor Shah Jahan as a symbol
of his love for his wife Mumtaz Mahal,
who died in childbirth.
Shifts of 22,000 men and women
worked 24 hours a day for 22 years
to complete the project.
Twenty eight gems, including jade and agate,
adorn the white marble building.
Magnificent solid silver doors and
a solid gold balustrade enclosed the tomb.
(They were later stolen by an enemy army.)
This monument of the Shah's love
for his wife is but a faint glimmer
of the Father's love for us.

How do I account for the Father's
incredible love for the human family?

To love another person
is to touch the face of God.
Finale of the musical *Les Miserables*

Week 9 — Day two

Journal

Jesus incarnates the Father's love

*God loved the world so much
that he gave his only Son,
so that everyone who believes in him
may . . . have eternal life.* John 3:16

The Lord says, "My thoughts . . .
and my ways are different from yours.
As high as the heavens are above the earth,
so high my thoughts and ways
are above yours." Isaiah 55:8–9
Consider one example of God's ways:
"When God wants a great job done
in the world or a great wrong righted,
He goes about it in a very unusual way.
He doesn't stir up His earthquakes
or send forth His thunderbolts.
Instead He has a helpless baby born,
perhaps in a simple home . . .
[to] some obscure mother.
And then God puts the idea
into the mother's heart,
and she puts it into the baby's mind.
And then God waits." E.T Sullivan

Why did Jesus choose this way of bringing his own son into the world?

*The mother's love is like God's love.
God loves not because we are lovable,
but because it is God's nature to love.
And because we are his children.* Earl Riney

Our faith reveals our Father's love

The Father himself loves you . . .
because you love me and have believed
that I came from God. John 16:27

A boy was born with an eye defect.
He could see clearly only nearby objects.
When the school told his parents that
he needed glasses, they ignored it saying,
"We didn't need glasses when we were kids.
Why should he?"
When the boy grew up, he went to an eye doctor.
After fitting him with lenses,
the doctor told him to look outside.
"Wow!" he gasped. "It's so beautiful!"
Later, he told author John Powell about
the episode saying: "That was the second-
most beautiful experience of my whole life."
Naturally, John asked him:
"What was the most beautiful experience?"
The boy said,
"When I came to believe in Jesus . . .
and saw that God is truly my Father . . .
and I felt the warmth of his love.'"
A Reason to Live! A Reason to Die, Argus, 1972

How seriously do I take Jesus?
How clearly do I see that God is my Father?

The measure of our love for God
depends upon how deeply aware
we are of God's love for us. Diodochus

Journal

Week 9   Day four

Journal

Jesus says, 'Love your enemies.'

*Jesus said, "You have heard it said,
'Love your friends, hate your enemies.'
But now I tell you: love your enemies."* Matthew 5:44

Kathryn Koob was terrified
when Iranian extremists took her hostage.
She writes: "As a diplomat, I was especially aware
that our government would not
give in to terrorists' demands."
So Kathryn put all her trust in God.
She says:
"I set about ordering my morning hours . . .
Bible studies, prayer and meditation . . .
I developed a morning prayer that went: . . .
'Thank you, Lord, for bringing me
through the night [and] giving me today. . . .
Show me what you would have me do.'"
She admits:
"There were a lot of days when it seemed
he wasn't having me do anything. But he was.
He was teaching me to love."
Finally, 13 months later, the ordeal ended.
Guideposts, July 1982

What motivates me to try to love enemies?

*If you love only the people who love you,
why should you receive a blessing?
Even sinners love those who love them.*
Luke 6:32

Day five — Week 9

Jesus teaches a surprising truth

*When the Son of Man comes as King . . .
he will say to those on his left . . .
"Whenever you refused to help
one of these least important ones,
you refused to help me."* Matthew 25:31, 41, 45

After graduating from Georgetown,
Anne Donahue volunteered a year
at New York's Covenant House,
a refuge for kids who wanted to quit the streets.
Every night she put hot chocolate and
sandwiches into a van and toured the city's
juvenile prostitution areas.
Anne says, "We're out there because
many kids haven't tried Covenant House yet.
We show the kids that somebody cares—
somebody not interested in exploiting them."
Anne says, "At first, I was very depressed.
What kind of God would let kids suffer so much?
Finally it hit me. God's not going to come down
and show us his love.
We have to let God's love shine through us."

What is one way in the last 24 hours
that I let God's love shine through me?

*Yours are the only hands
with which God can do his work. . . .
Yours are the only eyes
through which God's compassion can
shine upon a troubled world.* Saint Teresa of Avila

Journal

Week 9 — Day six

Journal

The Father loves us infinitely

The Father already knows what you need before you ask him.
Matthew 6:8

This prayer by Cardinal Newman focuses on God's intimacy in dealing with us:
"God calls you by your name . . .
and understands you . . .
God knows what is in you,
all your peculiar feelings and thoughts,
your dispositions and likings,
your strength and your weakness.
God views you in your day of rejoicing and in your day of sorrow.
God sympathizes in your hopes and temptations. God interests himself in all your anxieties and remembrances,
all the risings and fallings of your spirit. . . .
God hears your voice,
the beating of your heart
and your very breathing.
You do not love yourself better
than God loves you.
You cannot shrink from pain
more than God dislikes your bearing it."
(Slightly adapted)

What keeps me from knowing God better?

It is the heart that experiences God, not the reason. Blaise Pascal

Father, late have I loved you

[The prodigal son said,] "I will get up and go back to my Father." Luke 15:18

Late have I loved You,
O beauty ever ancient, ever new!
Late have I loved You!
And behold,
You were within, and I without,
and without I sought You.
And deformed I ran after these forms
of beauty You have made.//
You were with me, and I was not with You,
Those things held me back from You,
things whose only being was to be in You.//
You called; You cried;
and you broke through my deafness.
You flashed; You shone;
and You chased my blindness.
You became fragrant;
and I inhaled and sighed for You.
I tasted, and now hunger and thirst for You.
You touched me:
and I burn for your embrace. St. Augustine

How honestly can I pray this prayer?
What part of it speaks to me
in a special way? Why?

*To love and to be loved
is to feel the sun from both sides.*
David Viscott

Journal

Week 10 — *Plan of the Father*

Jesus' calling

William Blattey
wrote a fascinating novel called *Legion*.
In one scene a Jewish detective,
named Lt. Kinderman, is standing all alone
in a church in Washington, D.C.

He is there to investigate the case
of an old priest who was murdered while
hearing confessions.

Kinderman bends over and studies the blood
seeping out from the confessional
into the aisle.

After a while, he sits down in a pew,
wondering what kind of monster
would commit a crime like that.

He glances up at a huge crucifix on the wall.
As he studies it, his eyes come to rest
on the face of Jesus.
His own face softens
and a quiet wonder comes to his eyes.
He begins to speak to Jesus on the cross:

Who are you? God's son?
No, you know I don't believe that. . . .
I don't know who you are,
but you are Someone. . . .
Do you know how I know?
From what you said.

When I read, "Love your enemy," . . .
then I know that you are Someone.

No one on earth could ever say
what you said.
No one could even make it up.
Who could imagine it?
The words knock you down. . . .

Who are you and, what is it
that you want from us?

It was this same question
that many Jews asked on Good Friday night,
after hearing the reports
that Jesus had died on the cross.

It was the same question
that many Jews asked on Easter Sunday,
after hearing the reports
that Jesus had risen from the dead.
It is the same question
that every person in the world must ask
after reading the Gospel.

This week's meditations
focus on Jesus' own answer
to the question, "Who do you say I am?"

Day one — Week 10

'I am the bread of life.'

One day Jesus said to the people,
"I have come down from heaven
to do . . . the will of him who sent me.
What my Father wants is that all
who see the Son and believe in him
should have eternal life." John 6:35, 38, 40

Jesus went on to say to the people,
"I am the living bread
that came down from heaven. . . .
The bread that I give you is my flesh. . . .
Those who eat my flesh and
drink my blood . . . will live forever."
Many of Jesus' followers heard this
and said, "This teaching is too hard.
Who can listen to it?" . . . Because of this,
many of Jesus' followers turned back
and would not go with him any more.
So he asked the twelve disciples,
"And you—would you also like to leave?"
John 6:51–52, 54, 56, 60, 66–67

Who do I say Jesus is—and why?

The cup we use at the Lord's Supper . . .
when we drink from it,
we are sharing in the blood of Christ. . . .
And the bread we break:
when we eat it,
we are sharing in the body of Christ.
1 Corinthians 10:16

Journal

Week 10

Day two

Journal

'I am the light of the world.'

[One day Jesus was teaching in the Temple. He said to some Pharisees:]
"I am the light of the world.
Whoever follows me
will have the light of life
and never walk in darkness." John 8:12

Jesus went on to say:
"Whoever believes in me, believes not only
in me but also in him who sent me.
Whoever sees me,
also sees him who sent me.
I have come into the world as light,
that everyone who believes in me
should not remain in the darkness. . . .
I came not to judge the world,
but to save it. . . .
The Father who sent me
has commanded me what I must say
and . . . his command brings eternal life."
John 12:44–47, 49–50

In my own words,
what is Jesus saying to me about:
1) who he is, 2) who sent him, and
3) why he was sent?

Every action of our lives
touches on some chord
that will vibrate in eternity.
Edwin Hubbel Chapin

Day three Week 10

'I am the door for the sheep.'

Journal

*[One day Jesus healed a blind man.
The Pharisees expelled the man from the
synagogue for following Jesus, not them.
Jesus rebuked the Pharisees, saying:]
"The man who goes in through the gate
is the shepherd. . . .
The gatekeeper opens the gate for him;
the sheep . . . follow him,
because they know his voice."* John 10:2–5

Jesus went on to say:
"The sheep will not follow someone else;
instead, they will run away . . .
because they do not know his voice."
Jesus told the Pharisees this parable,
but they did not understand. . . .
So Jesus said again . . .
"I am the gate for the sheep. All others
who came before me are thieves. . . .
The sheep did not listen to them. . . .
Those who come in by me will be saved. . . .
The thief comes only in order to steal . . .
and destroy. I have come in order that
you may have life—life in all its fullness."
John 10:1–10

Identify the following in Jesus' parable:
sheep, thieves, gate, gatekeeper?

Life is a voyage that is homeward bound.
Herman Melville

Week 10 — Day four

'I am the Good Shepherd.'

Jesus said . . .
"I am the good shepherd,
who is willing to die for the sheep.
As the Father knows me
and I know the Father,
in the same way I know my sheep
and they know me." John 10:1, 14–15

Jesus went on to say,
"There are other sheep which belong to me
that are not in this sheep pen.
I must bring them, too; they will listen
to my voice and they will become
one flock with one shepherd.
The Father loves me
because I am willing to give up my life . . .
that I may receive it back again.
No one takes my life away from me.
I give it up of my own free will. . . .
This is what my Father
has commanded me to do." John 10:1, 14–18

Who are the "other sheep"
who listen to the shepherd's voice?
Besides listening to it in Scripture,
where else might they listen for it?

God talks to us at a level in ourselves
that we cannot reach . . . an inner dimension
that we didn't know we possessed
until he declared himself in it. Louis Evely

'I am the resurrection and the life.'

[Jesus arrived in Bethany, home of Lazarus, who had died four days earlier. Lazarus' sister Martha said to him:]
"If you had been here, Lord, my brother would not have died! But I know that even now God will give you whatever you ask." John 11:21–22

Jesus went on to say,
"Your brother will rise to life." . . .
"I know," she replied, "that he will rise
to life on the last day." Jesus said,
"I am the resurrection and the life.
Those who believe in me will live. . . .
Do you believe this?"
"Yes, Lord!" she answered. "I do believe . . ."
[Coming to the tomb of Lazarus,]
they took the stone away. Jesus looked up
and said, "I thank you Father,
that you listen to me,
but I say this for . . . the people here,
so they will believe that you sent me.". . .
Jesus called out . . . "Lazarus, come out!"
Lazarus came out. John 11:23–27, 41–43

How do I interpret Jesus' words and action?

In the night of Death,
Hope sees a star,
and listening Love can hear
the rustle of a wing. Robert Green Ingersoll

Week 10 — Day six

'I am the way, the truth, and the life.'

[Toward the end of his life, Jesus said,]
"Believe in God and believe also in me. . . .
After I go and prepare a place for you,
I will come back and take you to myself. . . .
You know the way that leads to the place
where I am going. John 14:1, 3–4

Thomas said to Jesus,
"Lord, we do not know where you are going;
so how can we know the way to get there?"
Jesus answered him,
"I am the way, the truth, and the life;
no one goes to the Father except by me.
Now that you have known me . . .
you will know my Father also . . .
You have seen him. . . .
Believe me when I say that
I am in the Father and the Father is in me.
If not, believe because of the things I do. . . .
Those who believe in me will do what I do—
yes they will do even greater things,
because I am going to my Father. . . .
I will do whatever you ask for in my name,
so that the Father's glory will be shown
through the Son." John 14:1–7, 11–13

How can we do "greater things" with Jesus?

Only when we learn to see the invisible,
will we learn to do the impossible.
Frank Gaines (slightly adapted)

'I am the real vine.'

*Jesus said, "I am the real vine,
and my Father is the gardener.
He breaks off every branch in me
that does not bear fruit, and he prunes
every branch that does bear fruit,
so that it will be clean and bear more fruit.
You have been made clean already
by the teaching I have given you."* John 15:1–3

Jesus went on to say,
"Remain united to me, and
I will remain united to you.
A branch cannot bear fruit by itself;
it can do so only if it remains in the vine.
In the same way you cannot bear fruit
unless you remain in me. . . .
Those who remain in me and I in them,
will bear much fruit. . . .
My Father's glory is shown
by your bearing much fruit;
and in this way you become my disciples. . . .
I have told you this so that my joy may be
in you and that your joy may be complete."

What are some ways that I remain
united to Jesus?

*Jesus said, "I have much more to tell you,
but now it would be too much for you to bear.
When, however, the Spirit comes . . .
he will lead you into all truth."* John 16:12–13

Journal

Week II — *Plan of the Father*

Our calling

Not long ago a woman
interviewed a young man from Argentina.
He had been held prisoner for six years
by the military government.

The young man had been tortured
and subjected to long hours of solitary.
The interviewer asked him
if he was bitter about his suffering
and the loss of six great years of his life.
He surprised her, saying:

*"I don't regard those six years as lost.
I took advantage of them
to strengthen my character and
to deepen my relationship with God."*

The young man's beautiful response
illustrates the words
of Paul in his letter to the Colossians:

*I am happy
about my sufferings for you,
for by means of my physical sufferings
I am helping to complete
what remains of Christ's sufferings
on behalf of his body, the church.*

Paul continues, saying

*I have been made a servant . . . by God,
who gave me . . . the task
of fully proclaiming the Father's message,
which is the secret he hid
through all past ages from all human beings but
has now revealed to his people. . . .*

*And the secret is that Christ is in you, which
means that you will share
in the glory of God.
So we preach Christ to everyone.*
Colossians 1:24–28

This week's meditations
focus on what Jesus said we must do
if we are to realize our lofty calling
to be disciples of Jesus.

Concretely,
this week's meditations deal with
how Jesus taught us to live
that we may bear fruit
and show forth the Father's glory.

Jesus says, 'Praise your Father in heaven.'

*You are like light for the whole world. . . .
Your light must shine before people,
so they will see the good things you do
and praise your Father in heaven.*
Matthew 5:13–16

In 1990, at the age of 71,
Nelson Mandela was freed after 27 years
of political imprisonment by enemies.
Three years later he won the Nobel Peace Prize.
The following year, he became
South Africa's first black president.
Mandela's spirit is captured
in these lines from his inaugural address:
"Our deepest fear is not
that we are inadequate. Our deepest fear
is that we are powerful beyond measure.
It is our light, not our darkness,
that frightens us.
We ask ourselves: who am I to be brilliant,
gorgeous, talented, fabulous? . . .
We are children of God. . . .
We were born to manifest the glory of God. . . .
It is not just in some of us.
It is in everyone."

Why can/can't I relate to Mandela's words?

*God loves man's lamplight
better than his own great stars.*
Rabindranath Tagore

Week II — Day two

Journal

Jesus says, 'Praise the Father by bearing fruit.'

Jesus said, "My Father's glory is shown by your bearing much fruit." John 15:8

The "Dear Abby" column for June 28, 1997, listed people who overcame obstacles to "bear much fruit" and thus, "give glory to their heavenly Father." A portion of it read:
"—Label him 'too stupid to learn,' and you have a Thomas Edison.
—Make him a 'hopeless' alcoholic, and you have Bill Wilson, founder of Alcoholics Anonymous.
—Tell her she's too old to start painting at 80, and you have a Grandma Moses.
—Tell a young boy who loves to sketch and draw that he has no talent, and you have a Walt Disney.
—Deny a child the ability to see, hear, and speak, and you have a Helen Keller."

What motivates me to keep going when I feel like quitting?

When things go wrong,
as they sometimes will.
When the road you're trudging
seems all uphill . . .
When care is pressing you down a bit,
Rest, if you must—but don't you quit.
Author unknown

Jesus says, 'Give as your Father gives.'

You know how to give good things to your children. How much more then, will your Father in heaven give good things to those who ask? Matthew 7:11

Few people
at Chicago's Children's Memorial Hospital
knew Gladys Holm by her name.
She was simply the "Teddy Bear Lady"—
the sweet old lady
who brought teddy bears to sick kids.
The hospital said the "teddy bears"
allowed Gladys to learn about families
who needed financial aid because of illness.
Then, she quietly took care of their needs.
Because she had no family
and had outlived her friends,
only a few people attended her funeral.
There weren't enough to carry the casket,
so a graveyard worker lent a hand.
No one guessed that hard work, investments,
and good luck enabled the "Teddy Bear Lady"
to amass a fortune of over $18 million.
She left it all to Children's—to help sick kids.

"Why we give is more important
than what we give." Anonymous
Why do I give?

*Not the person who has much is rich,
but the person who gives much.* Erich Fromm (adapted)

Journal

Week II   Day four

Journal

Jesus says, 'Forgive as your Father forgives.'

*Jesus said, "If you forgive others . . .
your Father in heaven will also forgive you."*
Matthew 6:14

A young man whose father had abandoned
his family was making a retreat.
He writes: "During one of the talks . . .
I visualized myself on my knees
before Jesus as he hung on the cross.
An enormous weight of guilt was upon me.
I wept for forgiveness.
As I wept, God forgave me . . .
He loved me in all my filth. . . .
I took the next day off from work
to think and to pray. While I was reading
the Bible, I began to think of my father. . . .
That night I went to his apartment
and asked his forgiveness for hating him. . . .
We hugged and kissed one another. . . .
I took a cab most of the way home
that night, but I wanted to walk
the last couple of blocks. Joy overflowed in me. . . .
With arms outstretched, I screamed,
"I love you, God!" He blessed me greatly
that night." Letter to the author

What keeps me from forgiving others?

We are like beasts when we kill.
We are like men when we judge.
We are like God when we forgive.   E.C. McKenzie

Jesus says, 'Be perfect like your Father.'

*Why should God reward you
if you love only the people who love you?
Even the pagans do that!
You must be perfect—just as your Father
in heaven is perfect.* Matthew 5:48

Mohandas K. Gandhi was the guiding star
and architect of India's independence.
For over 20 years he opposed British rule
with programs of nonviolent disobedience.
Toward the end of his life, he got many death
threats. This caused a friend to quip:
"The saints in heaven have been anticipating
Gandhi's arrival for sometime now,
but he's making them wait.
He's working on his dream of bringing
a bit of heaven's perfection to earth
before he leaves for heaven."
On January 30, 1948, Gandhi was shot
by an extremist, who didn't share his dream
of getting India's factions to live together
in mutual love and harmony.

What bit of heaven's perfection do I dream of
leaving on my own tiny strip of earth
before I depart for heaven?

*It is not a calamity to die
with dreams unfulfilled, but
it is a calamity not to dream.*
Benjamin E. Mays

Journal

Week II — Day six

Journal

Jesus says, 'I will witness for you.'

Jesus said,
"Those who declare publicly
that they belong to me,
I will do the same for them
before my Father in heaven." Matthew 10:32

One Sunday morning,
not long after the Civil War, a freed slave
wondered into a fashionable church
in Richmond, Virginia.
When the time for Communion came,
to the consternation of many present,
the ex-slave walked up to receive.
Sensing the mood of these people,
a prominent, respected man
walked down the aisle
and knelt next to his black brother.
That man's courageous witness
set an example that day that no one forgot.
The man was none other than Robert E. Lee,
former general of the confederate army.
Story told by Billy Graham

What are some of the things that keep me from witnessing to Jesus and his teaching in my everyday life?

Shine through me and be so in me
that every soul I come in contact with
may feel your presence in my spirit.
John Henry Newman

Jesus prays, 'Father, may they be one.'

*Jesus prayed: Father! May they be in us,
just as you are in me and I in you.
May they be one, so that the world
will believe that you sent me.* John 17:21

Bill Russell is a pro basketball legend.
He grew up in Monroe, Louisiana.
There his father worked long, hard days
in a paper bag factory.
But his father was a strong man, and would
return home each night still full of energy.
Bill writes:
"He'd call out to my brother, mother and me.
We would follow him to the fields
where the grass grew tall as wheat, and
the four of us would play hide-and-seek. . . .
When it was time to go home,
my father would reach down
and pick me up under one arm,
my brother under the other, lean down
so my mother could crawl up on his back,
and then run all the way home,
carrying his whole family,
as if we weighed nothing." *Second Wind, 1979*

How is this image of Bill's father an image
of God the Father and the human family?

***Father! To God himself we
cannot give a holier name.***
William Wordsworth

Journal

Week 12 — *Faith in the Father*

Call to trust

Every faith journey begins
with God knocking at the door of the heart.
The knock may be
a spiritual hunger in the soul,
a call to love in the heart, or
an illness in the body.

If we open the door,
God will sit down and eat with us.
God will then take us by the hand
and lead us—ever so gently—
into the unknown. Revelation 3:20

That brings us to "faith in God."

Faith—even at the natural level—
involves trusting another person.
For example, if a young lady tells us
she knows the telephone number
of a certain young man.
We don't have to "take her word for it"—
trust her—we can check it out
by calling the numbers she gave us.

On the other hand, if the same young lady
tells us that she loves a certain young man
and will be faithful to him all her life,
there's no way we can check this out.
We have to put faith in her.
We have to trust her and her word.
"Faith in God" is like that.

There is no way to "check out"
the "word of God" as it is revealed to us
through Moses in the Old Testament and
Jesus in the New Testament.

"Faith in God" also implies a new knowledge
about God, ourselves, and our world.
The nature of this new knowledge, however,
is that it can be had only by faith.
It cannot be "checked out"
It cannot be proved or disproved.
It can only be accepted or rejected.

This week's meditations.
focus on "faith in God."

"Faith in God" is that unmerited gift
given to us through the Holy Spirit,
that empowers us
to receive and to embrace
God's self-revelation to us.

All we can do is to open our hearts
to the "gift of faith."

This week's meditations
focus on the essence of faith:
trusting in God and God's word to us.

Day one — Week 12

What can I do to get the gift of faith?

Jesus said, "Believe because of the things I do." John 14:9, 11

The final day of school had ended.
The students had all gone home,
and the building was as quiet as a tomb.
A teacher was in her classroom,
picking up a few books that had been
carelessly or deliberately left behind.
Randomly, she picked up a book
that still looked usable.
It opened to this quote by Morris West:
"The sanctions of being a man
are so horrendous, that it seems madness
to try to relate them to
any kind of divine plane.
A cancer will eat your guts . . .
a drunken fool with an automobile
will mow you down . . .
The believers are the lucky ones . . .
But belief is a gift. . . .
If you have not the gift, you are just back
on reason."
In the margin a student had penciled,
"How does one get this gift?"
That single penciled sentence said it all.

How would you answer the student?

Faith is the light of the flame of love.
Poet Coventry Patmore

Journal

Week 12 — Day two

In my near-despair, I found the Father

Jesus cried . . . "My God, my God, why have you abandoned me?" Mark 15:34

Terry Anderson was kidnapped
by Shiite Muslim extremists in 1985.
He spent the next seven years
in Lebanon in windowless cells,
often in chains and in pain.
In December 1987, on the brink of despair,
he banged his head
against a wall until blood oozed out.
After release in 1992, he remarked
that some cynics deny God's existence,
saying, "We made him up out of our need,"
Then he observed,
"I only say that once in my own need
I felt a light and warm and loving touch
that eased my soul and banished doubt
and let me go on to the end.
It is not proof—there can be none.
Faith is what you have when you're alone
and find you're not." *Source unknown*

Explain Anderson's reason for affirming God's existence. Why do/don't I agree that we can't prove God exists?

*The LORD is near to those
who are discouraged;
he saves those who have lost hope.*
Psalms 34:18

In service to others, I found my Father

The person who is put right with God through faith shall live. Romans 1:17

A.J. Cronin began
his professional career as a physician.
Later he turned to writing.
In *Adventures in Two Worlds,* he says
that as a medical student he felt "superior"
to those gullible, uneducated folks
who still clung to "outworn myths."
He could only "smile" at their faith in the
existence of God and the human soul.
Then he adds:
"But when, as a qualified doctor,
I went out into the world,
to the mining valleys in South Wales and . . .
assisted at the miracle of birth
[and] sat with the dying
in the still hours of the night . . .
I lost my superiority,
and this, though I was not then aware of it,
is the first step toward finding God."

Why would this be the first step in finding God?
To what extent might it apply to my life?

I sought my soul—
but my soul I could not see.
I sought my God—but my God eluded me.
I sought my brother—and I found all three.
Anonymous

Journal

Week 12 — Day four

Journal

A voice said, 'Do you trust me?'

[A father asked Jesus to heal his child. Jesus replied,]
"Everything is possible
for the person who has faith."
The father at once cried out,
"I do have faith, but not enough.
Help me have more!" Mark 9:23–24

A man fell over the edge of a cliff.
Luckily, he managed to grab
a tree root about 10 feet below the edge.
He began to pray as he never prayed before.
Suddenly, a heavenly voice called out,
"Do you believe in me?"
The man shouted, "Yes! Yes! I do!"
The voice called out a second time,
"Do you trust me?"
The man shouted, "Yes! Yes! I do!"
The voice called out a third time.
"Alright, I'll save you,
but you must follow my instructions
and not ask any questions."
The man said, "I will! I will!"
The heavenly voice said, "Let go of the root."

In what sense is the story a kind of parable of what faith in God demands on our part?

Your faith . . .
does not rest on human wisdom
but on God's power. 1 Corinthians 2:5

Day five — Week 12

Jesus is my guide to the Father

Jesus said, "I am the way, the truth, and the life." John 14:6

Charles Lindbergh became the first person
to fly nonstop across the Atlantic Ocean,
landing in Paris in 1927.
A few days later, he flew to England
and was returning to Paris.
The visibility was bad and he lost his way.
Spotting a mail plane enroute to Paris,
he caught up with it, followed it,
and arrived back safely.
Lindbergh's adventuresome trip back
is a parable of our own life.
We are on a journey to the Father.
Like Lindbergh, we frequently get lost
and need a guide to trust and follow.
"Whoever follows me," said Jesus,
"will have the light of life." John 8:12

What keeps me from having greater
faith and trust in Jesus?

*I can see nothing plain;
all's mystery./
Yet sometimes there's a torch
inside my head/
That makes all clear,
but when the light is gone/
I have but images, analogies.*
William Butler Yeats

Journal

Week 12 — Day six

Journal

Faith is knowing with my heart

*Philip said to Jesus,
"Lord, show us the Father;
that is all we need."
Jesus answered,
"For a long time I have been with you all;
yet you do not know me, Philip?
Whoever has seen me
has seen the Father."* John 14:8–9

"The Christian faith
is firmly rooted in the incarnation,
in the conviction that God was in Christ
reconciling the world unto himself.
To believe in Christ
is to believe that God has come to earth
to dwell with us. . . .
Jesus is more than a religious genius
or a holy man or a spiritual pioneer.
To believe in Christ
is to believe that the living God has come."
Earle W. Crawford: Pulpit Preaching

What convinces me
more than anything else
that God, indeed, came to earth in Jesus?

In the movie, The Rainmakers,
Burt Lancaster says to Katherine Hepburn:
"You don't even know what faith is.
Well, I'm gonna tell you . . .
It's knowing with your heart."

Day seven — Week 12

Be glad when trials come

I do have faith, but not enough.
Help me have more! Mark 9:24

Saint Augustine was walking along a beach.
He was lost
in meditation on the central mystery
of Christianity, the Holy Trinity:
"How could God be three and one
at the same time?"
Suddenly, his attention was drawn
to a little girl carrying a small container
of water from the sea
to a hole she had dug on the beach.
What are you doing?" he asked her.
With childlike simplicity, she replied:
"I'm emptying the sea into this hole."
Then he stopped dead and thought:
"I am trying to do what that little girl is doing—
trying to crowd the infinite creator into
the finite creation of my little mind."

How might I be like the little girl at times?

[Be glad when trials come.]
Their purpose is to prove
that your faith is genuine.
Even gold, which can be destroyed,
is tried by fire; and so your faith,
which is much more precious than gold,
must be tested, so that it may endure.
1 Peter 1:6–9

Journal

Week 13 — *Faith in the Father*

An ongoing journey

A young person writes:
One day I committed my life to God.
This decision gave me great peace.
But two days later, I did something
no Christian would ever do.
I concluded that
I hadn't committed my life to God.
I'd only psyched myself into thinking I had.

This young person's experience illustrates a big mistake we can make about faith. We can think it is a one-time decision. Not so! Faith is an ongoing journey.

Psychology teaches us that the greater part of ourselves lies below our consciousness. This means when we commit ourselves to God, we commit only that part of which we are conscious. Thus, as consciousness of ourselves surfaces, we need to recommit this more mature vision of ourselves to God.

Another mistake we can make is to grow alarmed when our faith seems to eclipse or go behind a cloud for a while. Actually, this is normal and is usually traceable to our human nature, ourselves, or to God.

First, it may be caused by our human nature, which follows a rhythms of mood swings For example, one day we feel "up;" another day we feel "down."

Faith follows a similar rhythm. It simply goes with the territory of being human.

Second, an eclipse of our faith may be caused by ourselves. For example, we can neglect our faith and let it become weak because of sin or lack of spiritual food.

In other words, just as our body grows weak because of abuse or lack of physical food, so our soul grows weak because of sin or lack of spiritual food.

Finally, an eclipse in faith may be traceable to God, who allows it to happen in order to strengthen our faith. In other words, God uses trials to foster growth in faith. Take the case of Abraham.
When God asked him to sacrifice his son, Abraham was stunned!
"If I sacrifice Isaac," he thought to himself, "how can I have descendants through him?"
As a result, his faith was challenged.

Had Abraham said "no" to God, his faith would have been snuffed out. Instead, he trusted God and his faith grew and deepened.

This week's meditations focus on our never-ending faith journey to God.

I found myself without God

Do not abandon me, O LORD;
Do not stay away, my God!
Help me now, O LORD my Savior.
Psalms 38:21–22

A woman suddenly
found herself in a living nightmare.
She found herself in a world without God.
She felt that the floor of the world
had suddenly crumbled beneath her feet.
She was so stunned and destroyed
that she could hardly do more
than lay on a bed in a darkened room,
unable to think clearly or function.
She writes:
"I didn't want to see anyone.
I didn't want to see the light.
In truth, I didn't want to live."
Jean Toomer in Kerman and Elridge: The Lives of Jean Toomer, *1989*

Was there ever a time when my life turned
into a living nightmare? What caused it?
What helped me most to keep going?

Without God,
all our efforts turn to ashes
and our sunrise into the darkest of nights.
Without God,
life is a meaningless drama
in which the decisive scenes are missing.
Dr. Marin Luther King, Jr.: Speech c. 1963

Journal

Week 13

Day two

Journal

I don't believe the way I used to

Thomas said,
"Unless I see the scars of the nails
in his hands . . . I will not believe." John 20:25

A young person named Dan said:
"I don't know what's wrong with me.
I just don't believe like I used to.
At one time I believed a lot.
Now I don't seem to care any more."
Every young person,
at some point in life, has felt like Dan.
Commenting on this feeling,
John Kirvan says in *The Restless Believers:*
"The young person feels sick at heart;
he feels deeply guilty. Yet the chances are
that the only thing wrong with him
is that he's growing up. . . .
The youth is passing
from one stage of his life to another.
There is a kind of death involved.
The adolescent level of faith is dying,
so that the adult level can be born."

How comfortable am I with my faith
at this point in my life?

Those who think that a young person
is losing his faith merely because
he questions it, are missing the point.
To question is to care.
Anonymous

Day three — Week 13

God is not made out of wood

Jesus said:
"The time is coming and is already here
when, by the power of God's Spirit,
people will worship the Father
as he really is . . . God is Spirit,
and only by the power of his Spirit
can people worship him as he really is."
John 4:23–24

Leo Tolstoy
was a 19th-century social reformer,
religious mystic, and novelist.
Among his more famous novels
are *War and Peace* and *Ivan Ilyich*.
On the question of faith he said,
"If you cease to believe in
the God you once believed in,
there was something wrong
with your previous belief.
So you must strive to grasp better
that which you call God.
When a savage ceases to believe in
his wooden God, this does not mean
God doesn't exist. It only means
the true God is not made of wood."

What is my image of God?

Give me faith, Lord,
and let me help others find it.
Leo Tolstoy

Journal

Week 13 — Day four

Journal

Twice I turned back to my old ways

I will . . . go back to my Father. Luke 15:18

Dan Wakefield has won many awards
for his writing (e.g., *TV Guide,* NBC-TV, etc.)
But none of these awards filled the void
that he'd experienced
after he had left God behind in college.
Then, slowly, he began to turn back to God.
But the "return" road was not easy.
He writes:
"Twice I turned back to . . .
trying to numb my pain with drugs.
Throughout all this I never lost faith in God,
never imagined he was not there.
It was just that his presence was obscured.
Then the storm broke like a fever,
and I felt in touch again. . . .
I was grateful, but I also knew that
such storms . . . would come again."

How do I explain the "faith storms"
that so many Christians seem to experience?
How do I handle my own storms?

Faith is, after all,
an admixture of light and darkness.
We will always have enough darkness
to justify the refusal of light.
But we will always have enough light
to allow us to bear the darkness.
Louis Evely: *The Gospels Without Myth*

He pushed them and they flew

I do have faith, but not enough. Help me have more! Mark 9:24

Mary Rose McGeady
heads up the Covenant House organization.
It provides food, clothing, and medical care
for some 50,000 street kids.
She says that some of the most moving
prayers she's ever heard were prayed
by street kids in Covenant House chapels.
This happens when they gather to read
Scripture and pray in their own words.
The kids usually pray to forgive someone
or to be forgiven. She says a "spark
of faith" stays alive in many of these kids
despite what they've been through.
She adds that this spark can be fanned into
a flame, but it often takes a lot of patience
on the part of the one doing the fanning.

Do I know of a friend whose "spark"
of faith might be fanned to flame?
What might I do to help them?

Come to the edge.
No, we will fall.
Come to the edge.
No, we will fall.
They came to the edge.
He pushed them, and they flew.
Guillaume Apollinaire, French poet

Journal

Week 13 — Day six

Journal

Faith without love is nothing

*I may have
all the faith needed to move mountains—
but if I have no love, I am nothing.*
1 Corinthians 13:2

Cindy Pearlman of the *New York Times*
was interviewing actor Dustin Hoffman.
At one point, the two-time Oscar winner
joked about what to put on his tombstone.
One thing he'd thought about was:
"I knew this was going to happen!"
Hoffman is an artistic perfectionist.
Wolfgang Petersen, who directed Hoffman
in "Outbreak," says the actor would
phone him at three in the morning
about some idea for shooting the film.
The father of six,
Hoffman doesn't really care if his work
as an actor is remembered after his death.
What he'd like remembered
is his love for people, especially his family.
"That's what should go on your tombstone,"
Hoffman said. "Maybe mine should read,
'His family thought he was OK.'"

What does my family think about me?

*A house is built of bricks and stones
of sills and posts and piers,
But a home is built of loving deeds,
That stand a thousand years.* Victor Hugo

Father, help me to believe

*Then Jesus said to Thomas . . .
"Stop your doubting and believe."* John 20:27

Once, twins were conceived in a womb.
Together they explored it saying,
"How great is our mother's love
that she shares with us her very life."
Weeks passed; the twins began to change.
The first said to the second, "This means
our life in the womb is coming to an end."
The second replied, "I don't want it to end.
I want to stay here forever." The first said,
"But maybe there is life after birth."
The second replied, "How can there be?
We'll shed our mother's cord, and how is
life possible without it?" And so the twins
fell into doubt. "If life in the womb ends in
death," they said, "what's its purpose?"
And so the last days in the womb
were filled with confusion and fear.
Finally, the moment of birth came.
When the twins opened their eyes,
they cried for joy. For what they saw
exceeded their wildest dreams.

What is the point of this parable?

*What no one ever saw or heard,
what no one ever thought could happen,
is the very thing God prepared
for those who love him.* 1 Corinthians 2:9

Journal

Week 14 — *Presence of the Father*

Different ways

God spoke to us through three words: cosmic word *(creation),* inspired word *(scripture),* and incarnate word *(Jesus).*

God is also present in our world in three ways: *creation, scripture,* and *Jesus.*
God's presence in scripture (God's word), and in Jesus (God's Son) is fairly evident.
God's presence in creation (God's work) is not as evident.

God the Creator
may be compared to a movie projector.
As a projector creates all kinds of images,
God the Creator creates all kinds of things.
And as the images on the movie screen
would cease to be if the projector
withdrew its light from them,
so created reality would cease to be
if God withdrew his power from it.

Finally, as images on a movie screen
give a projector a *presence* on it,
so the things God created
give God a *presence* in our world.

This brings us back to the three ways
God is present in our world: through

— creation, which God sustains,
— scripture, which God inspired, and
— Jesus, whom God sent into our world.

These three ways that God is present to us
might be compared to the three ways
a son can be present to his mother: through
— an *artifact* that he made,
— a *letter* that he wrote, and
— in *person.*

The son's presence in the artifact
corresponds to God's presence in creation,
holding it in existence.

The son's presence through a letter
corresponds to God's presence in scripture.

And, finally, the son's presence in person
corresponds to God's presence in Jesus.

The different ways that God is present
in our world prompted the psalmist
to say of God's presence:

*If I went up to heaven you
would be there. . . .
If I flew away beyond the east
or lived in the farthest place in the west,
you would be there.* Psalms 139:7–10

This week's meditations
focus on God's threefold presence
in our world.

You are all around me

The LORD is . . . in this place, and I didn't know it. Genesis 28:16

During World War II, Eddie Rickenbacker
and a crew of seven crashed into the Pacific.
All supplies were lost,
except for four small oranges.
After eight days, it rained and they were able
to collect a supply of water to drink.
On another occasion, a seagull landed
on Rickenbacker's head.
He caught it for food, which they all shared.
After 21 days, rescue came.
One of the things that kept them going
was a prayer session each day.
A prayer they prayed often was Psalm 139.

Where could I go to escape from you?
Where could I get away
from your presence? . . .
If I flew away beyond the east
or lived in the farthest place in the west,
you would be there to lead me,
you would be there to help me. Psalms 139:7, 9–10

Can I recall a time when I seemed to sense
the Father's presence in a special way?

Closer is He than breathing,
nearer than hands and feet.
Alfred Lord Tennyson

Journal

Week 14 — Day two

Journal

I carry God's life within me

I will be with you always. Matthew 28:20

Joyce Rupp grew up on a farm. She writes:
"I had chores to do after school . . .
feeding the chickens and gathering eggs.
I didn't like doing this
because my free spirit wanted to be
out in the grove playing
or down by the creek watching tadpoles . . .
But one day all that changed for me.
I learned that I had a secret companion
who always kept me company, even when
I was doing the daily farm chores.
Hidden away deep within my heart
was a loving being named God who would
always love me and would never leave me.
It was at this time that a wise teacher
taught me about friendship with God.
She assured me that I would never be alone
because I was carrying
the very life of God within me."

Joyce Rupp: The Cup of our Life, Ave Maria Press, Notre Dame, Indiana, 1997, page 21

How aware am I of God's presence with me?

Fast falls the eventide.
The darkness deepens—Lord with me abide;
when other helpers fail and comforts flee,
help of the helpless—O abide with me!

Day three   Week 14

I felt God's loving presence

Journal

*Jesus said,
"Let the children come to me
and do not stop them."* Matthew 19:14

"I was five or six years old . . .
It was a calm, limpid summer morning . . .
The dew on the grass seemed to sparkle . . .
and the shadows of the houses and trees
seemed friendly and protective.
In the heart of the child that I was,
there suddenly seemed to well up
a deep overwhelming sense of gratitude,
a sense of unending peace and security
which seemed to be part of the beauty
of the morning."
The testimony ended by saying
that the friendly, protective presence
included "all that I had ever loved
and yet was something much more."
Quoted by Edward Robinson in *The Original Vision*
Seabury Press, New York, 1983

What is implied by the words "all that
I ever loved" and "something much more?"
What are some childhood experiences
I can recall, especially of a spiritual nature?

*Children know the grace of God
better than most of us. They see the world the way
the morning brings it back to them, new and born
and fresh and wonderful.* Archibald MacLeish

Week 14 — Day four

Train noises speak of God's presence

Come, let us praise the LORD! . . .
Listen today to what he says.
Psalms 95:1, 7

Louis MacNiece has a lovely poem
that describes how he found train sounds
mysteriously reassuring in his childhood,
as he lay in bed in the middle of the night.
Andrew Greeley says MacNiece's experience
gibes perfectly with his own.
He writes:
"My experience was the same as his—
the soft rumble waking me in the night
and the feeling
that somehow I was assured by the sound,
perhaps by the presence
of the outside world beyond my dreams . . .
Anyway, trains and train noises
are [to this day] a sacrament to me,
a sign of grace and transcendent presence."
Sacraments of Love, Crossroad, New York, 1994

What sounds do I remember as being reassuring to me in my childhood? What are some sounds at this time in my life that are for me "sacrament" of God's presence?

Everybody should have
his personal sounds to listen for—
sounds that make him . . . quiet and calm.
Conductor Andre Kostelanetz

'I experience God's presence in babies.'

Jesus said, "Unless you change and become like children, you will never enter the Kingdom of heaven." Matthew 18:3

After reading a magazine article about
how people find God,
Jean Shea asked her grade-school students
where they find God easiest.
One of the students, Allison Janik wrote:
"I find God in babies because
they express love, kindness, and gentleness.
Babies symbolize God
because babies are gentle and kind,
and can always make you smile. . . .
If you talk to babies and they don't
talk back, you still know they love you.
I think that's how it is with God."
Another student, Katie Drury, wrote:
"I find God through dogs,
because dogs are full of love. . . .
They always make you feel better . . .
and give you companionship,
just like God?"
James Martin, editor: *How Can I Find God,* Liguori Press, 1997

How do I find God most easily in my life?

*Every child comes with
the message that God
is not discouraged with us.*
Rabindranath Tagore

Journal

Week 14 — Day six

Journal

I experience God's presence in nature

*Jesus took Peter, James, and John,
and led them up a high mountain,
where they were alone. As they looked on
a change came over Jesus . . .
Peter spoke up and said to Jesus,
"Teacher, how good it is that we are here!"*
Mark 9:2–3, 5

Author Ardis Whitman cites
a remarkable episode from the files
of Abraham Maslow of Brandeis University.
A young mother was hurrying about
pouring coffee and juice
and spreading jam on toast.
Her husband was playing with their baby.
The other children were chattering away.
Suddenly, the mother
was so overwhelmed with the love
she had for her husband and children
that she had to fight back the tears.

When was a time that I was so overwhelmed
with joy that I had to fight back tears?

*The most important thing
about the people who've had experiences like
the mother is their conviction that
they have been privileged, momentarily,
with a vision of "the essence of things,
the secret of life, as if veils
had been pulled aside."* Abraham Maslow

Suddenly, I knew I wasn't alone

I thank you, LORD, with all my heart . . .
You answered me when I called to you;
with your strength you strengthened me.
Psalms 138:1–2

Years ago, New Mexico hot-air balloonist
Kathleen Baker-Gumprecht
ran into a serious problem in a stretch
of desert outside Albuquerque.
In the midst of the harrowing experience,
she found herself praying a psalm
that she had memorized as a child:
"Call to me when trouble comes;
I will save you, and
you will praise me." Psalms 50:7, 15
She said, "Suddenly I knew I wasn't alone.
I felt calm. Strength poured through me."
Fifteen minutes later,
she was on the ground, safe and sound.
That day, Kathleen discovered something
that millions of people today
would give anything to discover.

Why is it that many people,
who want to discover what Kathleen did,
do not discover it? How about me?

To the preacher who kept saying, "We must
put God in our lives," the Master said,
"God is already there. Our business is
to recognize this." Anthony De Mello

Week 15 — *Prayer to the Father*

Meditation

After playing basketball in a park,
I went to a nearby fountain for water.
The cool water tasted so good, and I felt
refreshment enter my sore, tired body.

Then I lay down and began to think.
"We need water to drink
But where does water come from?
Where does it come from?"
"Clouds!" I thought.
"But where do clouds come from?"
"Vaporized air," I answered.
This went on until I was left
with only one answer: God.

Then, I just lay on the grass
marveling at what God must be like.
Finally, I talked with God a bit
and started for home. Student (slightly adapted)

This prayer experience illustrates
the three forms prayer usually takes:

—meditation: thinking about God,
—contemplation: marveling at God,
—conversation: conversing with God.

Often these three forms
occur intertwined in the same prayer—
like strands of wire in the same cable.

Meditation is thinking about God or
God's presence or action in our world.
God's presence is like
TV signals that fill our atmosphere.
As a TV set is needed to bring these
signals into focus, so meditation is needed
to bring God's presence and action into focus.

Contemplation is marveling at God,
or God's presence and action in our world—
as the boy did in his prayer experience.
We are so struck by something about God
that we just rest there, saying nothing.
It is like lying on a beach, basking in the
beauty of the day and warmth of the sun.

Conversation,
is the simplest form of prayer.
It is talking to God from the heart—
as the boy did—and listening to God
speak to us in the depths of our being.

These meditations
focus on the first form of prayer:
meditation—thinking about God or
God's presence and action in our world.

Meditation on our earthly father

*God has decided
the number of the stars
and calls each one by name.* Psalms 147:4

Whittaker Chambers' book *Witness*
begins with a "Letter to My Children."
It describes some of his favorite memories
of their childhood. He writes:
"Sometimes, on a spring evening,
Papa would hear that distant honking . . .
and we would all rush out to see
the wild geese, in lines of hundreds . . .
head into the north. Or on autumn nights . . .
Papa would call you out of the house to . . .
watch the northern lights flicker
in electric clouds on the horizon . . .
till they filled the whole northern sky . . .
Thus as children you experienced
two of the most important things . . .
the wonder of life and
the wonder of the universe."

If one of my parents wrote me a letter
recalling two episodes from my childhood,
what might they be? Why these two?

*Disciple: Where must the seed be sown
       to bring the most fruit
       when it is grown?*
Master: Plant it in the heart of a child.
Author Unknown

Journal

Week 15 — Day two

Journal

Meditation on our heavenly Father

O LORD . . .
When I look at the sky,
which you have made,
at the moon and the stars
which you have set in their places—
what are human beings,
that you think of them . . .
that you care for them? Psalms 8:1, 3–4,

"I have been a night walker for years;
I love to contemplate the stars.
Their vastness evokes constant wonder. . . .
Some people tell me they feel small
when they look at the stars
and they don't like the feeling.
I feel small, too,
but I find it comforting. . . .
I want creation to be a lot bigger than me,
in part because I want the *Creator*
to be a whole lot bigger than me.
I need a God
whose ability to forgive, to love, to heal
are much greater than mine."
"Forward Day by Day" Edward S. Gleason, Ed.
Forward Movement Publications, 1997

How do I feel when I look at the stars?

The world will never starve for wonders;
but only for the want of wonder.
Gilbert K. Chesterton

Meditation on our Father's creation

O LORD, my God, how great you are!
You are clothed with majesty and glory . . .
and ride on the wings on the wind.
Psalms 104:1, 3

A young man describes his first sky dive:
"The plane door opens.
The spotter pats my back. I jump!
I strive for stability—the poetic arch.
I have it! I have it! I'm poetry in motion.
It's great! It's great!
I feel a jolt. My chute has opened up.
Tears blur my eyes. I thank God out loud!
Wow! What a beautiful place the sky is!
It's like a giant cathedral! It's God's place.
And more beautiful than I ever dreamed of!
It's a heaven here. Yes, a heaven!
I feel I'm dreaming.
But no dream has ever been so real.
I look down—to prepare for landing.
I ride the wind. I'm holding—facing the wind.
My landing is great!
Joy and pride well up inside me.
I'm a sky diver; and I'll never again
be the same." Mike Valentino (Adapted)

How do I explain the spiritual images
and echoes that leaped into the boy's mind?

The morning stars sang together and
all the sons of God shouted for joy. Job 38:7

Week 15

Day four

Journal

Meditation on respect for creation

*Jesus said, "Learn from me,
because I am gentle and humble in spirit."*
Matthew 11:29

Henry Ford put up a sign
on the front porch of his summer home:
"Please use the back door!
Phoebes are nesting in one corner;
robins in the other."
Author Jack Kytle traces Ford's respect
for nature to Ford's childhood.
One day, he was crossing a plowed field
with his farmer-father.
Coming upon a crooked furrow,
Henry asked,
"Dad, why isn't this furrow straight
like the others?"
His dad walked him over to a spot
in the field where a bird was nesting.
He said to Henry:
"I didn't want to disturb the mother bird,
so I just plowed around it."

How deep is my love for God's creation?
How do I manifest that love?

*Years ago, the newspapers reported
how a participant in a golf tournament
"let go his chance of winning,"
because he would not play his ball
out of a thrush's nest.* Anonymous

Meditation on our Father's power

*The LORD says,
"I will give you a new heart
and a new mind."* Ezeckiel 36:26

Life for 29-year-old Ron was a nightmare.
It followed a cyclic pattern of drugs,
crime, and prison. Then something happened.
Ron wrote from a prison cell in Boston:
"When I came to prison this time I was
tired of the lifestyle I had been living. . . .
I took advantage of education, recovery,
and counseling programs. . . .
I had to face all the hidden lies . . .
It wasn't until I fully accepted what I did
that healing could actually begin."
Something else, also, fueled Ron's healing.
It was the transformation of other guys.
He says: "You see them change completely.
You think . . . if they can change,
then there's hope for me. . . .
You begin to believe and know that there is
a greater power directing things because
you see that power reveal itself."
How Can I Find God? James Martin, editor

What is one thing I am struggling
to change in my life? With what hope?

*To repent and not to amend
is like paying a debt
by writing a check on water.* Anonymous

Journal

Week 15 — Day six

Journal

Meditation on our Father's mercy

Great is your constant love! Psalms 86:13

Frederick Faber's spiritual journey
was unusual, to say the least.
He grew up as a strict Calvinist,
was ordained an Anglican minister
and ended life as a Roman Catholic priest.
In his brief 49 years of life,
he wrote 150 hymns, like the following:
"There's a wideness in God's mercy,
like the wideness of the sea;
there's a kindness in His justice,
which is more than liberty.//
There's a welcome for the sinner,
and more graces for the good;
there is mercy with the Savior;
there is healing in his blood.//
For the love of God is broader
than the measure of man's mind;
and the heart of the eternal
is most wonderfully kind.//
If our love were more simple,
we should take Him at His word;
and our lives would be all sunshine
in the sweetness of our Lord."

How do I interpret the final stanza?

*While faith makes all things possible,
it is love that makes all things easy.*
Evan H. Hopkins

Meditation on Jesus' return to the Father

"Do not be worried and upset,"
Jesus told them. . . . "I will come back
and take you to myself." John 14:1, 3

Author Julie Houston used to sit with her sisters—
all under ten—on the seashore
shouting to their mother, "Come back!"
Their eyes were fixed on their mother
getting smaller and smaller as she swam out
into the ocean. All they could do was wait.
Then came the joyful moment.
Their mother would always turn and wave
to them reassuringly. Julie writes:
"This was the moment we hoped for.
We could not see her face but we knew
she was smiling, and that strong, confident arm
making wide arcs above the water
seemed to relay a solemn, motherly promise
that she would return.
She aways did, of course. . . running
up onto the beach smack into her children,
swarming around her with relief and joy,
rewarded for our trust by her wet, sandy hugs
and salty kisses."
Book of Eulogies, edited by Phyllis Theroux, Scribner, New York, 1997, page 239

How is this image of Julie's mother
similar to the image of Jesus,
shortly before ascending to his Father?

Little love, little trust. English proverb

Journal

Week 16: Prayer to the Father

Contemplation

You see things
vacationing on a motorcycle
in a way that is completely different . . .
[from vacationing in a car.]

In a car
you're always in a compartment and . . .
everything you see is just more TV.
You're a passive observer and
it is all moving by you in a boring frame.

On a cycle the frame is gone. . . .
You're in the scene, not just watching . . .
and the sense of presence is overwhelming.

That concrete
whizzing by five inches below your foot
is the real thing.
the same stuff you walk on.
Robert Pirsig: Zen and the Art of Motorcycle Maintenance

We might compare contemplation
to vacationing on a motorcycle.
It enables us to view God's creation
in a whole new way.

A good name for contemplation
is soul praying.
This style of prayer consists of simply
resting silently in God's presence.
Anthony Padavano
comments on contemplation this way:

A child
cannot say why a balloon fills him with joy;
a poet cannot find words
to match his wonder at the stars or the sea;
a musician is at a loss
to explain what Beethoven does to him.
a man in love
cannot express himself adequately. . . .

There are times
when words say nothing
and when silence expresses everything.
Belief in Human Life, Paulist Press,
New York, 1969

Resting silently in the Father's presence
helps us to become aware
of the activity of the Holy Spirit
in the depths of our being.
It helps us to listen
with the "ears" of the soul
to the "voice" of the Holy Spirit,
the gift of the Father and Jesus to us.

And so this week's prayer exercises
focus on *contemplation:*
marveling at God or
at God's presence and action in our world.

Contemplation on finding an acorn

Jesus said, "The Kingdom of heaven is like this. A man takes a mustard seed and sows it in his field. It is the smallest of all seeds, but when it grows up, it becomes the biggest of plants. It becomes a tree." Matthew 13:31–32

"I am a newspaperman, not a preacher . . .
God is off my beat. But one afternoon
I was walking across the yard
and stopped to pick up an acorn . . .
I could not tell you what Paul of Tarsus
encountered on that famous road to Damascus . . .
but I know what he felt.
He was trembling, and filled with astonishment,
and so was I that afternoon."
James J. Kilpatrick: Reader's Digest, April 1980

The reason why the newspaperman
was trembling and filled with astonishment
was the sudden revelation that the oak tree
under which he was standing
had grown from a tiny acorn—
like the one in the hollow of his hand.
Even more astonishing was the revelation
that from the tiny acorn,
an entire planet could be forested.

What in nature do I find most astonishing?

Be still, and know that I am God.
Psalms 46:10 RSV

Journal

Week 16

Day two

Journal

Contemplation on lying on a beach

*As the sun was rising,
Jesus stood at the water's edge,
but the disciples
did not know it was Jesus.* John 21:4

A deserted stretch of beach
is one of the most peaceful places on earth.
The surf, washing the beach,
has a way of silencing the hectic rhythms
of schedules and timetables.
"One falls under their spell, relaxes,
stretches out prone. One becomes . . .
like the elements on which one lies,
flattened by the sea . . . erased by today's
tides of all yesterday's scribblings.
And then, some morning in the second week,
the mind wakes, comes to life again . . .
It begins . . . to turn over in gentle careless rolls
like those lazy waves on the beach.
One never knows what chance treasures
these easy unconscious rollers
may toss up on the smooth, white sand
of the conscious mind."
Anne Morrow Lindbergh: *Gifts From the Sea*

What is a "chance treasure" that I found recently during a "time of quiet"?

*There is no prayer so blessed
as the prayer which asks for nothing.*
O. J. Simon

Day three — Week 16

Contemplation on a beautiful Sunday

*[We went] to the beach
where we all knelt and prayed.* Acts 21:5

Last Sunday about ten of us
went up to my family's cottage on
Lake Michigan. It was a cool day,
so we went to the beach fairly well clothed.
Toward the end of the afternoon
we built a fire and watched the sunset.
Next day, I learned that one of my friends
left some clothes at the cottage.
So I went back by myself to get them.
When I got to the cottage, I ate lunch,
and walked along the beach.
When I came to where we had built the fire,
I saw the piece of driftwood
on which one of the girls
had carved all of our names.
The feeling of yesterday filled me,
like an echo.
I picked up the driftwood, brought it back,
and gave it to the girl to keep for all of us,
as a remembrance of a beautiful Sunday.

What "remembrance" of a beautiful time
do I possess?

*May you never forget
What is worth remembering
Or remember
what is best forgotten.* Irish Blessing

Journal

Week 16

Day four

Journal

Contemplation on rainy days

The storm makes my heart beat wildly. . . .
God sends lightning across the sky . . .
and torrents of drenching rain.
He brings our work to a stop. Job 37:1–2, 6–7

As a boy,
Frederick Buechner loved the rain.
He loved the feel of it on his face and legs.
Above all, he wrote:
"I loved the sound of it on trees and roofs
and window panes . . . I loved the hiss
of rubber tires on rainy streets
and the flip-flop of windshield wipers.
I loved the smell of wet grass and raincoats
and shaggy coats of dogs.
A rainy day was a special day . . . a day when
the ordinariness of things was suspended . . .
and even people transformed . . .
as the rain drew them closer."
Frederick Buechner: *The Sacred Journey*

Why do rainy days draw us closer?
Why does this hold true
for "figurative" rainy days as well?

How beautiful is the rain!
After the dust and heat,
In the broad and fiery street,
in the narrow lane,
How beautiful is the rain.
Henry Wadsworth Longfellow

Contemplation on cherry trees

*He decided the number of stars
and called each by name.
Great and mighty is our Lord.* Psalms 147:4

A.J. Cronin was a physician and novelist.
He eventually gave up medicine to devote
fulltime to writing. He authored such books
as *Hatter's Castle* and *Keys of the Kingdom*.
One afternoon, during a visit to Italy,
he drove to a famous monastery in Florence.
After wandering around the grounds
for a while, he came upon an old man
and began conversing with him.
The man had a gentle soul and, in spite
of being "bent with toil and rheumatism,"
had a bright sparkle in his eye.
At one juncture in the conversation,
the old man pointed to an orchard,
which was his special care and smiled:
"I see my cherry trees in bud,
and then in flower, and then in fruit.
And then I believe in God."

What strengthens my "belief in God?"

*Who on a still summer night dare gaze
upward at the constellations . . .
without the overpowering conviction
that such a cosmos came into being
through something more than blind chance?*
A. J. Cronin: *Adventures in Two Worlds*

Journal

Week 16 — Day six

Journal

Contemplation on a miraculous rescue

The LORD who created you says, "Do not be afraid—I will save you . . . I have called you by name—you are mine." Isaiah 42:1

On Christmas Eve 1983, Tim Anderson and two college roommates were driving from Connecticut to Chicago. The car radio warned against going outside, because a windchill of 80 below had hit the Midwest. The boys dropped off one roommate in Fort Wayne and took off by a rural route to the Indiana tollway. Miles from nowhere, their car choked, sputtered, and died. No lights could be seen anywhere. As the frigid cold invaded their car, the desperate boys began to pray for help. Suddenly, lights appeared out of nowhere— a tow truck. It took them back to their friend's house in Fort Wayne. Tim ran inside to get money for the tow fee. When Tim returned, he stopped dead. No tow truck was in sight—and only one set of tire tracks was in the snow: their car's.
Digested from Joan Webster Anderson's *Where Angels Walk*

How firmly do I believe that God can and does hear our prayers?

If I don't pray with confidence, how can I hope to receive that for which I pray? Anonymous

Day seven — Week 16

Contemplation on faces of the poor

Jesus said,
"Happy are those
who know they are spiritually poor;
the Kingdom of heaven belongs to them."
Matthew 5:3

Helen Prejean
has served as a spiritual counselor
to prisoners on death row since 1982.
Her best-selling book, *Dead Man Walking,*
became a popular Hollywood film.
In an interview, James Martin asked her
where she, personally, finds God in her life.
She replied:
"The most direct road I have found to God is
in the faces of poor and struggling people . . .
And that brought me
straight into the execution chamber. . . .
In that situation, I experienced
a tremendous *strength* and presence of God."
How Can I Find God, James Martin, editor

Why would the faces
of poor and struggling people act as a map
showing a direct road to God?

We come closest to God
in our lowest moments. . . .
It is painful to get to that point,
but when you do, God is there.
Terry Anderson, 5 years as a hostage in Lebanon

Journal

Week 17   *Prayer to the Father*

Conversation

Eight-year-old Jamie was dying of cancer. Occasionally, when his mother heard him talking out loud, she hurried to his room. Finally, on one such occasion, he said:

Mom, you don't have to get up every time you hear me. Sometimes I'm just praying and talking to God. . . .

When his dad asked, "Does God talk back to you when you talk to him?" Jamie . . . quietly explained, "Dad, I don't hear God with my ears. He answers me in my heart."
Tina D'Alessandro: *A Journey Home,* America, August 16, 1997

Jamie's response to his dad illustrates a common form prayer takes: conversing with God
Of these two activities, listening to God is, by far, the least understood.

Normally, "listening to God" involves communication via one of five faculties: mind, will, emotions, memory, imagination. A brief explanation of each might help:

God enlightens our *minds,* enabling us to discern a proper course of action.
God strengthens our *wills,* enabling us to pursue a difficult course of action

God calms our *emotions,* enabling us to act in a controlled way.

God jogs our *memories,* enabling us to access an experience that God can use as a vehicle to initiate faith, strengthen faith, or fan to life a smoldering faith.

Finally, God stirs our *imaginations,* enabling us to see new approaches. For example,
In George Bernard Shaw's play, *St. Joan,* the following dialogue takes place:

Joan: I hear voices telling me what to do. They come from God.
Robert: They come from your imagination.
Joan: Of course. That is how the messages of God come to us.

A concluding caution: It goes without saying that we can't equate every movement of a faculty as coming from God. Prayerful discernment and spiritual direction are sometimes needed to make clear which movements are from God and which are not.

This week's prayer exercises focus on conversing with God.

Conversation with an elusive Father

Who are you, Lord? Acts 9:5

Father, I don't know if I know you or not.
They say you're closer to me
than I am to myself.
But that's not the way it seems to me.
Is this, perhaps, where I lose the trail,
looking for you the way I picture you,
rather than the way you are?
Should I even look—
can the eye ever see the eye?
Could it be that while I walk in flesh,
you will never be a destination—
only a journey?
What if I found you?
That would be heaven!
But can heaven be on earth?
When does the quest cease to be
a question and become the answer?
Or, perhaps, that is it:
the question is the answer,
the search is the discovery.
For in searching, I am already there—
as "there" as any searcher can ever be.

What is the point of the final line?

Whoever seeks Truth,
praises the Beautiful,
or loves the Good, is really—
though he know it not—close to God.

Week 17   Day two

Journal

Conversation with an obliging Father

Ask God for what you need, always asking him with a thankful heart. Philippians 4:6

A magazine article entitled "Coincidence or Miracle?" listed several "coincidences" that seemed to go beyond the normal meaning of the word.
Just before the magazine went to press, editor Richard Reese received a letter from a rancher in Oregon.
He told how one day he set out across his ranch with the sole purpose of doing some serious praying. At one point he prayed to God: "I know you love me, but it would be nice sometimes if you would 'tell' me so."
Minutes later, he noticed a small object reflecting the sun brilliantly. He said:
"It looked like a wadded-up piece of tin foil, but when I picked it up I realized it was an old Mylar balloon that had floated in from who knows where. As I slowly unfolded it, my heart raced. There, in large letters, were the words 'I Love You' surrounded by red roses." Catholic Digest 7, 1997

To what extent do I agree that "a coincidence is a small miracle where God chose to remain anonymous?" Heidi Quade

Seek the Lord while he may be found,
Call on him while he is near. Isaiah 55:6

Conversation with a protecting Father

Suddenly a fierce storm hit . . . and the boat was in danger of sinking. Matthew 8:24

Sixteen-year-old Robin Lee Graham sailed from Los Angeles in July, 1965 on a 24-foot sloop called *Dove*. His only companions were two kittens and a guitar. Thirty thousand miles later, he crossed the Los Angeles breakwater. Reporters were waiting with questions. Robin answered, "Yes, I've memories enough for a lifetime." "Yes, there were times when I thought I might be crazy—like the night a storm swept *Dove's* deck clean." An entry in his journal for October 13 read: "I was leaning forward when a huge wave rocked *Dove*. I thought she might capsize. Flying objects hit me. . . . The sea broke in a portlight, and green water poured in below. Luckily, I was able to wedge the Plexiglass back into its frame. Otherwise, the seas might have swamped me. . . . That night, I prayed to God . . . long and hard."

When did I face serious danger? How did God strengthen *my will* to face it courageously and *my mind* to face it intelligently?

"You're sailing alone? You must be crazy!"
"Around the world? You'll never make it!"
Actual remarks to Robin, after he would dock in seaports.

Journal

Week 17 — Day four

Journal

Conversation with an unknown Father

The father at once cried out,
"I have faith, but not enough." Mark 9:24

Years ago, *The Song of Bernadette*
was a best-selling book.
The story behind it is noteworthy.
The famous Jewish writer Franz Werfel
and his wife fled the Nazis,
hoping to get to Spain and sail for America.
Denied entry into Spain,
they took refuge in Lourdes, France,
home of the famous shrine to Our Lady.
The first night there, Werfel went
to the shrine and prayed in effect:
"I am not a believer . . .
But on the chance that God is real,
I ask for your help.
See us to safety and I will write the story
of this place for all the world to read."
Later, he told Fulton Oursler,
senior editor of the *Reader's Digest:*
"After making that prayer,
I experienced a deep and profound peace."
Within days, Werfel and his wife found a way
to America and he kept his promise.

What keeps me from asking God's help
with greater confidence?

Prayer is releasing the energies of God. Author Unknown

Conversation with an everlasting Father

O LORD . . . you were eternally God and will be God forever. Psalms 90:1–2

Isaac Watts' paraphrase of Psalm 90 celebrates God's presence and action in our world in these words:
"O God, our help in ages past,
our hope for years to come,
our shelter from the stormy blast,
and our eternal home.//
Under the shadow of Thy throne
still may we dwell secure;
sufficient is Thine arm alone,
and our defense is sure.//
Before the hills in order stood
or earth received her frame,
from everlasting Thou are God,
to endless years the same.//
Time, like an ever rolling stream,
bears all its sons away;
they fly, forgotten, as a dream
dies at the opening day.//
O God, our help in ages past,
our hope for years to come.
Be Thou our guide while life shall last,
and our eternal home."

How have I experienced God's help recently?

If God is for us, who can be against us?
Romans 8:31

Journal

Week 17

Day six

Journal

Conversation with a compassionate Father

Jesus said, "Come to me, all you who are tired from carrying heavy loads."
Matthew 11:28

"Every morning before school,
a friend and I used to jog together.
On Saturday mornings, we'd jog longer,
take a break about halfway through,
sit down and talk about our problems.
Both of us looked forward to these talks.
Then one morning she didn't show up.
After school I went to her house and
found her family preparing to leave the city.
Next day, I picked up the newspaper.
On the front page was a terrible story.
My friend and her family were killed
in a head-on collision.
Eventually, time healed this wound.
But time has never changed one thing.
Whenever I have an extra-heavy problem,
I jog out alone. Halfway through,
I stop, sit down, and talk out
my problem, as if she were with me.
I always jog home refreshed and at peace.
Anonymous high school boy (adapted)

How are the boy's "talks" an ideal image of an ideal form of prayer?

Prayer is talking something over *with God, not talking God out of something.* Anonymous

Conversation with an ever-loving Father

*Jesus went up a hill to pray
and spent the whole night there
praying to God.*
Luke 6:12

Each night the sufi poet, Rabi'a
said a prayer that went something like this:
"My Lord and my God:
eyes are closed; stars are quiet in the sky;
the movements
of birds in their nests
and of fish in the sea
are at rest . . .
The door of the king's palace
is bolted and
the king's sentries stand guard.
But your own door, my Lord and my God,
is unlocked and open to receive
all who approach you.
And so at this hour, each lover
is alone with his beloved and
I am alone with you, my Lord and my God."

What is one prayer I say each night
to "my Lord and my God"?

*O Thou who art at home
Deep in my heart,
Enable me to join you
Deep in my heart.*
The Talmud

Journal

Week 18 — *Prayer to the Father*

The Psalms

The Book of Psalms
has been called Israel's Soul Book.
This is because it played such a major role
in Israel's worship of the Father.

The Book of Psalms
is both a *prayer book* and a *hymn book*.
It gives us a glimpse into how
Israel prayed and sang to the Father
in times of doubt, sorrow, and joy.

Tradition divides the psalms
into themes: praise, wisdom, royal,
thanksgiving, and lament.

Praise psalms focus on the *Father's glory*.
They usually begin with words like
"Praise the LORD!" Psalms 150:1

Wisdom psalms focus on *human conduct*.
They usually begin with the words
"Happy are those." Psalms 41:1

Royal psalms concern the *king*.
Starting with the promise to David,
that a Messiah would come into his line,
the king of Israel became
more than a political figure.
He became a religious symbol as well.

Each new king brought Israel closer to
the "King of Kings," the promised Messiah.

And so psalms were composed to celebrate
important events in the king's life.
Take Psalm 101.
It sounds like the king's oath of office:

*I will live a pure life in my house
and will never tolerate evil. . . .
I will destroy the wicked in our land.* Psalms 2–3, 8

Thanksgiving psalms express *gratitude*
to God for benefits and blessings:

*You have changed my sadness
into a joyful dance;
you have taken away my sorrow
and surrounded me with joy. . . .
I will give you thanks forever.* Psalms 30:11–12

Finally, *lament* psalms are *"songs of woe,"*
in which the psalmist pours out his heart
to God about some situation, such as defeat
or injury at the hands of an enemy:

*I am like a lonely bird on a housetop.
All day long my enemies insult me.*
Psalms 102:7–8

This week's meditations
focus on the psalms and how they can be
applied to situations in our own day.

Father, hear my cry for help

I look to the mountains,
where will help come from?
My help will come from the LORD,
who made heaven and earth. Psalms 121:1

Mary Rose McGeady is President of Covenant House. Each year nearly 50,000 homeless kids show up at Covenant House. Usually enmeshed in a web of abuse and sex, they are as young as ten.
For these kids, Covenant House is often the "last ray of hope" in a dark world that few of us will ever know or see.
In *Please Help Me, God,* Mary Rose gives us a taste of life in Covenant House. Here's a kind of "modern psalm" written by one of her "street children:"
"Help me, Dear Lord,
as I travel towards You.
There are many detours
which will try to distract me from you.
Help me as I travel my path . . .
Help me though I may fall,
to continue my journey towards You.
Help me, Dear Lord.
I want so much to be with You."

What is my attitude toward kids like this?

He has the right to criticize
who has the heart to help. Abraham Lincoln

Journal

Week 18 — Day two

Journal

Father, help me to start over again

*From the depths of my despair
I call to you, LORD. Hear my cry.*
Psalms 130:1–2

If you sat in a Covenant House chapel,
here's what you might see.
Now and then, a kid will walk in,
go slowly to the front of the chapel.
The kid puts a slip of paper in a special box,
called a "prayer box."
It contains a heartfelt prayer to God.
It sounds like a "modern psalm."
Here's an an actual example:
"Dear Heavenly Father . . .
Give me the wisdom . . . . to do
what is right and not wrong. . . .
I know I haven't been making the right decisions,
but I'd like to better that.
Life has not been easy . . .
but I know that you will give me
the strength to go on, for I do believe in you
and all you say and do."
Rose McGeady: *Please Help Me, God*

What prayer ought I to write out
and put in that "prayer box" right now?

*Oh, help me, Lord, to take the time
To set all else aside,
That in the secret place of prayer
I may with you abide.* Author Unknown

Father, don't stay away from me

"My God . . . why have you abandoned me? . . .
Don't stay away from me!
Come quickly." Psalms 22:1, 19

Marion Bond West lost her father
when she was about four years old.
This made it necessary for her mother
to take a job to support her. So her mother
arranged to have a neighbor baby-sit Marion.
Each lunch hour Marion's mother
hurried home to eat with her. But when she
left after lunch, Marion grew hysterical.
One day Marion's mother stopped coming.
Years later, Marion learned why.
Her mother still came each noon,
sat at the window, watched her play,
and longed to hold her close—especially
when she fell and cried.
But for Marion's own good, she didn't.
This story helps us understand why God
sometimes seems to withdraw from us—
even for long periods. It's for our good:
to help us mature and deepen our faith.
Marion Bond West: "Close By" *Guideposts*, June 1979

How does God's apparent withdrawal
serve to mature and deepen our faith?

Everywhere that we can be,
Thou, God, art present there.
Isaac Watts (Slightly adapted)

Journal

Week 18

Day four

Journal

Father, give me a loving heart

*Happy the person who honors the LORD . . .
Light shines in the darkness . . .
for those who are merciful.* Psalms 112:4

Defeated German soldiers were being marched
in single column through Moscow.
First came the Nazi officers—
well-fed, well-dressed, heads held high.
Their demeanor was one of superiority
to their ill-clothed onlookers—
mostly angry,
Russian women who had lost sons
and husbands in the fierce fighting.
Next came the German soldiers—
young, thin, ill-clothed, hobbling on crutches,
heads hanging in pain and shame.
The street went deathly silent at the sight.
Then an old woman took a crust of
dry bread from her pocket and gave it
to a young soldier, who could hardly walk.
(It may have been her own evening meal.)
Then other women began giving the wounded
soldiers bread, cigarettes, and kerchiefs.
These soldiers were no longer enemies.
They were suffering human beings.
Reported by Donald Nicholl in *Triumphs of the Spirit in Russia*

How hard is it for me to look at suffering
enemies and see suffering human beings?

*You may call God love . . . but the best name
for God is compassion.* Meister Eckhart

148

Day five Week 18

Father, be a lamp to guide my feet

Journal

*Your word is a lamp to guide me
and a light for my path. . . .
You are my defender and protector . . .
Hold me and I will be safe.* Psalms 119:114, 117

Kap Shik was teaching scripture
in a Christian high school in South Korea
in June of 1950.
Then on June 25th, the Korean War broke out.
As North Korean troops poured across
the 38th parallel and invaded South Korea,
thousands of South Korean citizens,
including Kap and his family, evacuated
their homes and fled deeper into south.
Kap left behind a library of expensive books.
Many of of them had been paid for
by skipping meals and going hungry.
When Shik's family fled, however,
the only book they took was the Bible.
Kap wrote later:
"Every evening while we were on the road,
our family read the scriptures.
Amongst the threat of war and its anxiety
and uncertainty, the Bible gave us hope."

What does the Bible mean to me? Why?

*I know the Bible is inspired
because it finds me
at a greater depth of my being
than any other book.* Samuel Taylor Coleridge

Week 18 — Day six

Journal

Father, you forgive the sins of my youth

Teach me your ways, O LORD;
make them known to me.
Forgive the sins
and errors of my youth. Psalms 24:4,7

The headline of an article
in the Louisville *Courier-Journal* read:
"Science Writer Gallant
Recalls Flunking Chemistry."
The article explained that nine years ago
Roy A. Gallant failed organic chemistry
at Bowdoin College. Now he'd just won
the Thomas Alva Edison award for his book,
Exploring The Universe.
He said that his interest in science writing
developed after leaving school.
He also made this confession:
"When I went to high school . . .
I fancied myself a poet.
I used my physics book as a prop
to conceal poetry I wrote during class."
Gallant is now studying for his Ph. D.
at the Columbia Graduate School
of Journalism.

What impact does failure have on me?

God's grace within me
and God's strength behind me,
can overcome any hurdle ahead of me. Anonymous

Father, you heard my cry for help

I waited patiently for the LORD's help; then he listened to me. Psalms 40:1

Helen Hayes was one of Hollywood's most respected stars. At one point in her career, everything went right. Nothing went wrong. Life was one excitement after another. The upshot was that she drifted slowly from "formal religion and closeness to God." Then tragedy struck. Her daughter died. Now everything seemed to go wrong. Nothing seemed to go right. She turned to God; but God wasn't there. Her situation went from bad to worse. She began to despair. Then, one night, after hours of tossing and turning, she got up, turned to Psalm 40, and read: "I waited patiently for the LORD's help; then he listened to me and heard my cry." She wrote later: "I waited patiently from that moment on . . . I understood that faith comes of itself, not by straining after it." Then, one day, God was there again, and peace returned to her soul.

Toward what/whom am I most impatient?

Patience is accepting a difficult situation without giving God a deadline to remove it.
Author Unknown

The Lord's Prayer–I

One day
Jesus was praying in a certain place.
When he had finished,
one of his disciples asked him,
"Lord teach us to pray." Luke 1:1

Jesus responded
by teaching them the "Lord's Prayer."

"This, then, is how you should pray:

Our Father in heaven:
  May your holy name be honored;
  may your kingdom come;
  may your will be done on earth as
    in heaven.
  Give us today the food we need.
  Forgive us the wrongs we have done,
  as we forgive the wrongs that others
    have done to us.
  Do not bring us to hard testing,
  but keep us safe from the Evil One."
Matthew 6:9–13

Apart from the fact
that Jesus taught us the "Lord's Prayer,"
what is unique and special about it?
St. Augustine answers this way:

The Lord's Prayer
is the most perfect of prayers. . . .
In it we ask, not only for all the things
we can rightly desire, but also the sequence
that they should be desired
This prayer not only teaches us
to ask for things, but also in what order
we should desire them.

The "Lord's Prayer" contains seven petitions.
They divide into two parts.
The first three petitions
have the *Father* as their focus:

—*your* holy name,
—*your* kingdom come,
—*your* will be done.

The last four petitions have *us,*
God's children, as their focus:

—give *us,*
—forgive *us,*
—bring *us* not,
—keep *us* safe.

These meditations
focus on the seven petitions
of the "Lord's Prayer."

Father . . .
your holy name be honored

Jesus prayed at the Last Supper:
"Father . . . Give glory to your son,
so that your Son may give glory to you."
John 17:1

Author Ardis Whitman presents
a beautiful example of what we mean by
"glorifying" or "hallowing" God's name.
One summer afternoon a musician
was standing on the tower that marks
the highest peak of the Mohawk Trail
in the Berkshire Mountains.
"Three states—Connecticut, Massachusetts,
and New York—spread before them . . .
valleys, forests, and lakes.
He was so moved by the grandeur of it all
that he ran to his car, grabbed his cornet,
and climbed back up the tower.
There he played with all his heart—
for his own delight, for the other tourists,
and for the glory of God.
"This, Too, Is Worship," *Reader's Digest,* May 1982

How do I glorify or hallow God's name best?

To lift up the hands in prayer
gives God glory, but a man with a dungfork
in his hand, and a woman with a slop-pail,
give him glory, too. God is so great
that all things give him glory
if you mean they should.   Gerard Manley Hopkins

Journal

Week 19

Day two

Journal

Father . . . your Kingdom come

*Jesus went to Galilee
and preached the Good News from God . . .
"The kingdom of God is near!"* Mark 1:14–15

For centuries, Jews gathered in synagogues
to read the scriptures and
pray for the coming of God's kingdom.
Then, one day,
Jesus began preaching,
"The Kingdom of God is near!" Mark 1:15
The phrase "kingdom of God" did not mean,
primarily, a nation like other nations.
Rather, it meant an "action of God"
within the hearts of people.
That action would arrest the tide of evil and
begin the process of bringing all hearts
into union with the Father's will.
The process would be a "long one,"
because the forces of evil would resist
with an all-out "life-and-death" struggle.
Jesus announced that the beginning
of this long process was at hand.

What is the status of God's kingdom
in my heart? What is the chief obstacle
to establishing God's kingdom there?

*Wherever God
rules over the human heart as King,
there is the kingdom of God established.*
Paul W. Harrison

Father . . .
your will be done

*Jesus said, "Not everyone who calls me
'Lord' will enter the Kingdom of heaven,
but only those who do what my Father . . .
wants them to do."* Matthew 7:21

The night before Martin Luther King, Jr.
was shot on a balcony of the Lorraine Motel
in Memphis, he gave a stirring speech
in Birmingham, Alabama.
It was prophetic of the tragic event
that took place the next day. He said:
"Well, I don't know what will happen now. . . .
Like anyone, I would like a long life.
Longevity has its place.
But I'm not concerned about that now.
I just want to do God's will.
And He's allowed me to go up the mountain;
and I've looked over, and I've seen the
promised land. I may not get there with you,
but I want you to know tonight,
I'm not worried about anything.
I'm not fearing any man.
Mine eyes have seen the glory
of the coming of the Lord."

To what extent can I say truthfully,
"I just want to do God's will?"

*We do not resign ourselves
to the will of God; we relate ourselves
to God's will.* Author unknown

Journal

Week 19

Day four

Journal

Father . . . give us today our daily bread

*"I am the bread of life,"
Jesus told them. "Those who come to me
will never be hungry."* John 6:35

In his book *Swimming in the Sun,*
Albert Haase tells how one afternoon,
he was walking through the grounds
of the infamous Dachau concentration camp.
Coming to the spot where Barracks 26
once stood, he paused and prayed.
That barracks was the prison dormitory
where many Catholics were imprisoned by
the Nazis in World War II.
Each day they were given one meal,
consisting of a chunk of bread and
a cup of watered-down soup.
Each day one of the prisoners
sacrificed their meager bread ration
to make possible the celebration of Mass.
This "daily bread" ration was then
secretly consecrated by a priest and
passed around as communion for prisoners.

How willing am I to sacrifice what
I have that others may receive
their physical or spiritual "daily bread"?

*The effect of our sharing
in the body and blood of Christ
is to change us into what we receive.*
Pope St. Leo the Great

Day five — Week 19

Father . . . forgive us as we forgive

"I will get up and go to my Father and say, 'Father, I have sinned.'" . . . So he got up and started back to his father. Luke 15:18–20

A college student named Rex was often rude to others and critical of them. But because he had a great voice, the chaplain asked him to be in the choir for Good Friday. During the service, the chaplain spoke about Jesus' crucifixion. After Holy Week, Rex began to change. The change was so great that a friend asked him about it. Rex said: "It all began when the chaplain said that Jesus died for me. That made me wonder if I was worthy of such a sacrifice." Then Rex fell silent. Finally he said, "I have always been ashamed of my father, who is in prison. Because of what the chaplain said, I've decided to live my own life and try to become worthy of Jesus' sacrifice."
Marion Ash: "The Touch of the Master's Hand," Canadian Messenger of the Sacred Heart, September 1997

What keeps me from living my life fully?

The great gift of being a human being lies in our freedom to continually right our wrongs and make new persons of ourselves.
Wang Yang Ming

Journal

Week 19

Day six

Journal

Father . . . do not bring us to hard testing

Jesus said, "Keep watch and pray that you will not fall into temptation." Matthew 26:41

Former TV celebrity Walter Cronkite
grew up in Texas.
One day, he asked a store if he could buy
a watch and pay for it a little at a time.
When he told his mother what he had done,
she made him return it, saying:
"Your intentions are honorable, Walter,
but even you admit you don't know
how you're going to earn the money. . . .
There's no dishonesty here,
but it's one of those risky gray areas."
Guideposts, "Words To Grow On," April 1988
That story helps clarify the petition,
"do not subject us to the final test."
Scripture says God tempts no one. James 1:13
God does, however, allow trials to come
our way. So if we don't "watch and pray,"
these trials could "subject us to the final test,"
in the same sense that Walter Cronkite's mother
warned him that his arrangement could do so—
if he wasn't careful.

Have I ever gotten to the point
where a trial became so overwhelming
that I was led to the brink of temptation?

*Better shun the bait
than struggle in the snare.* John Dryden

Father . . .
keep us safe from the Evil One

O God . . . I have sinned against you . . .
Put a new and loyal spirit in me.
Psalms 51:1, 4, 10

One night, young Thomas Merton was blessed
with an awareness of the evil within him.
He was alone in his room.
Suddenly, he was overwhelmed
at the thought of the evil in his soul.
His whole being rose up in revolt against it.
He wanted to be delivered from this evil
with an urgency and intensity
he'd never experienced before in his life.
He writes in *The Seven Storey Mountain:*
"For the first time in my whole life
I really began to pray—
praying not with my lips and
with my intellect and my imagination,
but praying out of the very roots of my life . . .
to the God I had never known, to reach down
towards me out of His darkness and to help me
get free of the thousand terrible things
that held my will in their slavery."

How well can I relate to this experience?
Can I recall a concrete example?

True repentance hates the sin,
and not merely the penalty; and it hates
the sin most of all because it has discovered
and felt God's love. William M. Taylor

Journal

Week 20: Prayer to the Father

The Lord's Prayer–2

The son of a wealthy father had everything
he ever wanted, except a brother.
He used to talk to his Father about this.

Then one day
the father adopted a poor, orphan boy
about the same age as his own son.

From the start the two boys got along,
as if they were blood brothers.
Both were happy beyond all belief

One afternoon they were outside
tossing a football.
The adopted boy stopped for a minute
and said to his new brother:

"Gee, I wish my old friend Danny
had a football like this.
He likes football and is really good at it,
but his father can't afford a football.

The adopted boy's new brother said,
"Why don't you ask "our Father"
to get him one?

The adopted brother said,
"But I couldn't do that.
He's given me so much already,
I couldn't ask him for more."
Then his new brother said,
"Don't forget, Danny,
'my father' is now 'your father'.
He is 'our father!'

He wants you to share with him
your every desire and need.
If he thinks it's something
that will be for your good, he'll give it to you—
just as he gives me things for my good.

Suddenly, the adopted son realized
what a wonderful father he had.
At that moment,
his relationship with his father
took a giant leap forward.

That story
is a kind of parable of God the Father,
our brother Jesus, and ourselves.

Because of Jesus
we can now call God "Our Father"
and approach him
with total trust and confidence.

This week's meditations
focus once again on the only prayer
Jesus ever taught us: the Lord's Prayer.
It is a summary of the key things
that we should know about "our Father".

Father . . .
your holy name be honored

Praise the LORD. Psalms 150:1

"I sing the mighty pow'r of God
that made the mountains rise,
that spread the flowing seas abroad
and built the lofty skies.
I sing the wisdom
that ordained the sun to rule the day;
the moon shine full at His command,
and all the stars obey.//
I sing the goodness of the Lord
that filled the earth with food;
He formed the creatures with His word
and then pronounced them good.
Lord, how Thy wonders are displayed
where'er I turn my eye;
If I survey the ground I tread
or gaze upon the sky!//
There's not a plant or flow'r below
but makes Thy glories known;
and clouds arise and tempests blow
by order from Thy throne.
While all that borrows life from Thee
is ever in Thy care.
and ev'rywhere that man can be,
Thou, God, art present there.

What deed of God makes me want to sing?

*God has his own secret stairway
into every heart.* Anonymous

Journal

Week 20　　　　　　　　　　Day two

Journal

Father . . .
your Kingdom come

[At last judgment, the king will say,]
"Come, you that are blessed by my Father . . .
possess the kingdom." [To the wicked
he'll say,] "Away from me." Matthew 25:34, 41

Picture yourself walking along—
with healthy eyes on a brilliant spring day.
Beauty and God seem to be everywhere.
You say: "This must be what heaven is like!"
Now, picture yourself walking along—
with sick eyes on the same day.
It pains you greatly to open your eyes.
And so you see neither beauty nor God.
You see only pitch-black darkness.
An early Christian teacher, Gregory of Nyssa,
used this example to illustrate
the difference between heaven and hell.
The sunlight stands for the face of God.
The healthy eyes stand for you—
if you've cultivated the spiritual ability to look
into God's face. The sick eyes stand for you—
if you've freely refused to cultivate it.
Gregory's point is this. God hasn't changed;
you have. Nor does God "punish" you;
you do that by your own free choice.

How am I preparing for the coming of God's
Kingdom by cultivating my spiritual ability?

As much of heaven is visible
as we have eyes to see. William Winter

Father . . .
your will be done

*Our Father . . . May your will be done
on earth as it is in heaven.* Matthew 6:9–10

One night a young man was home alone.
He began thinking about his life.
Suddenly, he saw himself as being
selfish and self-centered. He was shocked!
Next, he turned his thoughts from himself
to all the suffering people in the world.
He began feeling compassion for them.
Then, he did something that surprised
even himself.
He knelt down and told his heavenly Father
that he wanted to change his life.
The next morning when he awoke,
he had a sudden illumination. He writes:
"I knew that love and service of mankind
was the *will* of God . . .
We are to serve God by serving his purpose. . .
My whole outlook on life changed . . .
It was as if all my life
I had been in a darkened room and then
I had suddenly walked out into the sunlight."
Alister Hardy: The Spiritual Nature of Man,
Clanendon Press, Oxford, 1979

How consciously and sincerely do I pray
in the Lord's prayer, "Thy will be done"?

*Jesus prayed, "Father . . . not my will . . .
but your will be done."* Luke 22:42

Week 20　　　　　　　　　　Day four

Journal

Father . . . give us today our daily bread

Jesus said, "I am the living bread that came down from heaven." John 6:51, 58

One stormy night, two boys came to the
rectory of Chicago's Holy Family Church.
They wanted a priest for a dying woman.
Father Damen followed them through
the rain to an old house.
The boys stayed downstairs, while Father
went upstairs, anointed the woman,
and gave her Communion.
The woman asked Father, "Who sent for you?"
He said, "The boys." She said, "What boys?
I live alone; and no one knew I was dying."
When Father Damen described the boys,
she was shocked. They fit the description
of her boys, who had been altar servers
at Holy Family and had died in a flu epidemic.
When Fr. Damen went downstairs
to find the two boys, they had disappeared.
To commemorate this amazing episode,
Father Damen placed two statues
of altar servers in the sanctuary of
Holy Family. They remain there to this day.

What does this story celebrate?

Behind the dim unknown,
Standeth God within the shadow,
keeping watch above his own. James Russell Lowell

Day five   Week 20

Father . . . forgive us as we forgive

Journal

*Jesus said, "If you forgive others . . .
your Father in heaven
will also forgive you."* Matthew 6:14

Keith Miller committed his life to God.
Later, he wrote in *Taste of New Wine:*
"I had to find out
what this God is really like
to whom I had committed my future.
I realized that my closest relationships
have always been with those who knew
the most about me, and loved me anyway.
So I began to reveal my inner life to God . . .
(even though I knew God already knew) . . .
After making a total . . . confession,
I thanked God for His forgiveness."
But, then,
Keith discovered something disturbing:
he could not forgive himself for some sin.
And so, one day
while praying with a close Christian friend,
he confessed the sin aloud to God.
Then he was able to accept God's forgiveness.

Is there anyone
that I am finding it hard to forgive?
What might I do about this?

*She hugg'd the offender,
and forgav the offense.*
John Dryden: *Cymon and Iphigenia*

Week 20 — Day six

Journal

Father . . . do not bring us to hard testing

*Suppose there are brothers and sisters
who need clothes
and don't have enough to eat.
What good is there in your saying to them,
"God bless you!"*
James 2:16

Thomas Merton accepted Christ at age 23.
At 26, he gave away all his possessions
and entered a Trappist monastery
in Gethsemane, Kentucky.
There he became a priest and an author.
His books include his autobiography,
The Seven Storey Mountain,
and *Seeds of Contemplation,*
a book on Christian living. In it he writes:
"It is easy enough to tell the poor
to accept their poverty as God's will
when you yourself have warm clothes
and plenty of food
and medical care and a roof over your head
and no worry about the rent.
But if you want them to believe you . . .
share some of their poverty and see if you
can accept it as God's will yourself."

How willing am I to do that?

*A lot of people are cheerful givers,
but only when their giving advice about
what others people should do.* Anonymous

Father . . .
keep us safe from the Evil One

*I call you friends
because I have told you everything
I heard from my Father. . . .
I have much more to tell you,
but it would be too much for you to bear.
When, however, the Spirit comes . . .
He will give me glory,
because he will take what I say
and tell it to you."* John 15:15, 16:12–14

Dr. Lloyd Judd practiced medicine
in rural Oklahoma. Many of his patients
were poor and had no transportation.
He often drove to their homes in the middle
of a cold night to treat them,
knowing they couldn't pay him.
One day, he took sick, went to a hospital,
and learned that he had terminal cancer.
His thoughts turned to his children.
He had much that he wanted to tell them,
but they were too little to understand it.
So he recorded a set of tapes for them.

In what sense is Dr. Judd's recording
of the tapes for his children
similar to Jesus' gift of the Lord's Prayer
to his followers?

*The Lord's Prayer is quickly committed to memory,
but it is slowly learned by heart.*
Author unknown

Journal

Other Books in this Series

JESUS: Meditations for the Millennium
HOLY SPIRIT: Meditations for the Millennium

Other Books by Mark Link

Bible 2000

Challenge 2000

Vision 2000

Mission 2000

Action 2000

For further information call or write:
Thomas More®
An RCL Company
200 East Bethany Drive
Allen, Texas 75002–3804

Toll Free   800–264–0368
Fax   800–688–8356

Daily Meditation Format

Begin each meditation with this prayer:

Father, you created me
and put me on earth for a purpose.
Jesus, you died for me
and called me to complete your work.
Holy Spirit, you help me
to carry out the work
for which I was created and called.
In your presence and name—
Father, Son, and Holy Spirit—
I begin my meditation.
May all my thoughts and inspirations
have their origin in you
and be directed to your glory.

Follow this format for each meditation:

1. READ the meditation prayerfully.
   (About one minute.)
2. THINK about what struck you most
   as you read the meditation. Why this?
   (About four minutes.)
3. SPEAK to God about your thoughts.
   (About one minute.)
4. LISTEN to God's response.
   Simply rest in God's presence
   with an open mind and an open heart.
   (About four minutes.)
5. END each meditation by praying the
   Lord's Prayer slowly and reverently.